NEVER
BEEN
PUNCHED...

NEVER
BEEN
PUNCHED

By Neil Bird

To Tony.
It don't mean becoming a wuss!
Enjoy the Book
Neil Bird

silverlensmedia
Somerset · England · United Kingdom

DEDICATION

Dick and Annie Brummitt

The vision we have for the future has brought this great friendship together. The journey is young and we have lots to do. I loved this quote by the author Bill Johnson in his book 'The Supernatural Power of a Transformed Mind' he said 'It's an unprecedented time to be **Alive**, and you and I get to be a part of it.' How true that is!

I'd like to extend this dedication also to my entire family, biological and spiritual. Thank you for your support and encouragement. You have helped me through some tough times and made me laugh during the good times. I am chuffed to bits that I can share my life with you lovely bunch!

CONTENTS

FOREWORD

The Ancient Greeks would say 'The glory of a young man is in his strength'. It is good to have physical strength, but is it this that really makes a man?

Neil Bird had his fair share of strength and he knew how to use it. As you read this book Neil demonstrates his prowess using both brawn and brain.

As with all journeys in life, there are ups and downs, pains and sufferings, heartaches and happiness. Neil tells of his, both eloquently and honestly, but through it all it was on 'his terms' and 'his strength'. The question is, how long could his life continue like this?

Eventually Neil realised his strength and intelligence (a university graduate as well!!) could not sustain him. A broken marriage, many jobs, friends and associates, all would let him down and disappoint.

Then came the time when Neil opened his heart to God, who would never let him down and would give him the ultimate source of strength. Strength to make the right decisions, strength to stand up for what is right in life, strength to look at himself and to give him, in a word, 'integrity'. I believe it takes a stronger man or woman, no matter how young or old, rich or poor to do what is right. With God's help, as with Neil, He can do that for us all.

I pray you enjoy reading Neil's story and watch out for future writings from him as his life progresses down a very different path with God.

Respect and regards

Arthur White
Member & Trustee of 'Tough Talk'

INTRODUCTION

Welcome to my first attempt at writing, and hopefully the first of many. I have plenty to share both in experiences and things I have learnt along the way. I want to share this with you as it will entertain you, challenge the way you think and open your eyes to a dark world some of you may not even know exists.

I had the amazing pleasure of the company of two people during my time studying in Bradford in 2008. These people were writing their own books and were both an amazing encouragement to me to get on and do it. The thing is, what I am really buzzing to tell you, will have to be in book two, as my eventful life has stepped up a whole new level and is becoming even more exciting. In this first book, I feel it's important to introduce myself to you, in order that you get an understanding of who I am, where I came from and what I got up to. I think my colourful past will make a great read for you.

Here's a bit of background for the psychoanalytical bunch. Those who like to understand the background to help them try and suss out what makes me the man I am today. So, in a nutshell, I was born and bred a Somerset lad. I had a major dislike for school life, but in general, childhood was good and I had a good relationship with my parents, even though they split up when I was a teenager. As a result of their divorce, I chose to leave home at 15 years of age, where I moved into a local YMCA hostel and grew up fast. I drank the local brew when out with my mates, as well as other concoctions, of which I have no memory, probably best that way. So, in general, apart from living on my tod very early on, I had a good life. Skint for most of it, but in general all was good. This is the nutshell of my life, not the nut itself but I do feel I have shared enough for now. So whether you think I was a messed up kid with potential problems or not, as the 1990's disco-diva Gloria Gaynor put it, 'I am what I am!'. I'm starting to sing it as I type.

I'll be honest at the outset and explain the reason for this vague account of the past, this is due to a strange lack of memory. I guess I tend to focus on the future instead of the past and any memories shared in this book have been dug out after much thought. Some fond memories include the youth group I attended in my teens, but even then, most of this is vague. Friends have shown me photos of myself in my late teens and it still doesn't jog my thoughts. There's one picture I remember seeing recently, where I was sat with a team of young technicians for a youth multimedia event. Although I recognise the venue, I have no memory of the occasion at all. I remember the top I was wearing, but that's about it. I used to think it's a shame, because there are lots of things I got up to as a young lad, but now I find the future so exciting that it no longer bothers me that I have gaps in my memory of the past. When I mentioned this to a friend as a minor concern, they replied by telling me that God shields off the bad memories from me, in order to keep my focus on looking forward. This was an idea I liked the sound of.

A few weeks before starting to write this book, some friends on the course I was on challenged me to go without caffeine for a week. Just a week I thought, that sounds achievable, I could do that. What a mistake to make. I'm no health freak, so the number of coffees was reaching about ten a day. The reason they challenged me was because of my nocturnal lifestyle. I could easily stay up till the early hours and still get up for studies in the morning. I have more hours in the day than most, only requiring about six to seven hours of sleep. There was another reason for this challenge. A student friend, also known as the biggest Jaffa cake fan on the planet, was currently going a month without biscuits. His name is Errol. I have to confess, I plated up a pyramid of Jaffa cakes to try and get him to crack. I have the utmost respect for this guy. He made it through a whole month without a single biscuit. Ok may be not the utmost respect, but at least a tad of respect for doing it. But Errol was one of those who challenged me along with one other who felt the lack of caffeine would bring out the true side of my character, expecting me to crack. Nice friends, but I like a good challenge. For me, a week without caffeine was harder than I thought. I stopped on the Friday at 5.30pm and by Saturday evening I had a headache. This headache stuck around all week and didn't budge. Whenever I bent over, my head pounded. Although tired and in pain, I had no bad temper or grumpiness, which did surprise the challengers. They were disappointed when on Friday at 5.30pm the following week, I kick-started the caffeine with two strong filter cups in half an hour. I was buzzing all night and the headache eased by about 9pm. I am telling you all this because, as a coffee lover, this book has been completely fuelled by caffeine and written over many quiet nights and afternoons in coffee shops. If any coffee shops would like to sponsor the next book by keeping me well stocked with coffee, I'm cool with that, but it has to be strong stuff. You know the sort, the stuff a teaspoon can stand up in.

In February 2008, I bought a children's cartoon DVD with the Bible story of Jonah. Oh man have I changed, there was a day when the only DVDs I bought had an 18 certificate on them. My movie collection had a mix of stars from Al Pacino, Bruce Willis and I'm ashamed to own up to it, Steven Segal. Most films had plenty of explosions, some form of martial arts, guns and a high body count. There was a day I'd call myself an action junkie. Anyway, when I began to write this book, I had about three references to the story of Jonah from random sources and I began to realise this Bible story of making choices about your direction, is similar to my life. Another character in the Bible I can identify with is a man named Job. Similarities can be seen from his story as you begin to read chapter seven.

My life is an example of personal radical change. I remember a Church leader once said, 'The Church of tomorrow is wrapped up in the decisions you make today!' One day in 2006, my life changed. You are about to read up until this point. This is the background of my life; the dirt that was cleansed and my sins, the things I had done wrong, which were forgiven. God gave me a second chance.

By now you should be getting a feel of how I write. I write as I talk and enjoy expressing my thoughts in pictures for people to understand. This should make this an enjoyable read. However, as the book title suggests, I now feel this would be a good time to warn the sensitive reader. The theme of the book is of an adult nature due to the environment it is set in and not really suitable for the younger reader. I've chosen not to include the swear words that occurred on a frequent basis, I hope this doesn't remove the attitude and shock factor of the situations. There is violence, drugs and lots of drunken people. Those who prefer not to know about this side of the world we live in need to stop reading now. Those who continue may be shocked to know that the Neil Bird you know and love, had a dark past. Welcome to my world.

'WHAT HAVE I GOT MYSELF INTO'

'WHAT HAVE I GOT MYSELF INTO'

One hundred miles south east of Bridgwater, where I am now based, is the student hub of the south coast, Southampton. It was 1997, and I was moving there to commence my degree studies in Human Resource Management for three years. My fiancé, Tina, was studying there on a four-year degree course. She had already done a year, so when I turned up to start my studies it meant that we'd finish at the same time. We were due to finish in the summer of 2000, when we planned to get married. Seemed like a good idea being the millennium and all that.

Moving to Southampton was easy. I drove there in April time, met up with Tina and a few others and went house hunting for when I began the course. Tina and her female student friends were already in halls of residence until the summer, then needed to look for student housing in the city. We all got in our cars and drove off to the nearest newsagents to pick up a local rag, to look through the 'To Let' section. I had a letter to post and needed some stamps and saw a small corner shop with a post office counter. As I went in, Tina went to the newspaper section to pick up the local paper and I went to the post office counter to buy my stamp. I spoke with the cashier behind the glass and asked him whether he knew of any landlords in the area. Now then, amazing as it sounds, he was one and offered to take us for a viewing at 2pm that afternoon. Well how about that, one enquiry and we had a viewing arranged. We drove to a local estate and viewed a place that was advertised in the newspaper. We saw it from the outside and decided not to even go in, the local area was enough to put us off. For an hour or so we sat around making a few phone calls and drinking coffee. Most places were already taken and others seemed a tad high in rent. So, we got back in the cars and drove off, with our A-Z of Southampton, to find the address for our two o'clock viewing with our post office landlord. As we drove into the cul-de-sac, our jaws dropped. The entrance had pillars with globes on the top. It had classic street lamps and the buildings were no older than five years old. We were driving into an upper class area where the cars on the drives were either Mercedes or Jaguars. There I was, driving in the cul-de-sac with my blue and rust coloured two-door mini with four people inside.   Forget about what the neighbours must have thought when they saw us pull in, think about the suspension, it's only a mini.

When we stood in the centre of the cul-de-sac we looked at the properties and thought we'd been set up. We were thinking that this guy was having a laugh when we walked into his post office asking for accommodation. These houses were estimating around a quarter million in value.

It was past 2pm and we were really beginning to think this was a wind-up and started to walk back to our car when this little Daihatsu Hi-jet van sped into the cul-de-sac. It was the post office guy. He got out and introduced himself as Mr Singh. This seemed so unlikely we couldn't believe what was happening. He showed us around this luxury abode and we immediately fell in love with it, well who wouldn't, our only question was... 'How Much?'. The rent was high but after some brief negotiation I was able to get him down £250 to £1000 a month. We had four rooms, one for me and three for the girls. The landlord wasn't concerned with who was there just that the rent would be paid. The house soon filled up with a total of six in the house. Tina's friends had boyfriends who also moved in. This made the rent much easier as we shared it between six of us.

We'd landed ourselves a posh residence, where our neighbours on one side used their house as a summerhouse, as they lived in South Africa. On the other side we had a professional retired couple paying good money to be there. What they were not best pleased about, was their new student neighbours. What a great experience, I'll be surprised if I'm in a posh residence like that ever again. It was three good years. We were good with the rent each month and had good relations with our landlord.

I moved into the house in August, two weeks before the others. It was a nice quiet time before the excited bunch of students came. This was a good time to look for a job and get the utilities sorted for the house. I bought newspapers and applied in the usual way with application forms for jobs. Getting no replies, I began to think I needed to hit the streets and see what was out there. I visited a pub where I sat at the bar with a newspaper and a pint of John Smith's Smooth. I tried to chat to the barman, but conversation was a struggle. The barman was not really interested in general chit-chat. Have you ever sat in a bar on your own with little interaction from the bar staff? I felt awkward, I felt like a complete stranger in an un-welcoming city. I built up the courage to ask the barman, after explaining where I had come from and what I was doing in the town.

'Do you know if the managers looking for security for this place?'

'No, the managers not the one to ask, you want a security group, they're always looking for new guys,' said the barman.

I asked if he knew of any or had a directory to look up a number. He pointed me to a company called Pro-Security. I dialled the number on my mobile and after a brief interview over the phone, the time and place was arranged for an interview in person. When I hung up, I couldn't believe it was that easy. I was chuffed to bits that within a few days of being in Southampton, I'd moved in, found a job and was excited about my new student life ahead of me. I asked the barman for another pint and continued to chat to him for a while about the area, what entertainment was about for nights out and spoke more about what I was going to be studying.

The day of the interview had arrived and I set off in my old faithful mini. Not the best impression to give off, but hey it's a set of wheels. I had no idea where I was going. All I had was an address and the local A-Z. When I got to the destination, I was slightly puzzled. It was a newly built detached house, I guessed it must have been his house. It had a big metal 6ft gate at the entrance, like it didn't expect visitors. I parked on the roadside and entered the gate. Walking up to the door I felt a tad nervous. I knocked on the door and waited. It was a big house, so I waited a bit more. The big white door opened about a foot, a man's head peered around the door.

'Not the front door, go to the side gate and walk on through into the garden,' he said.

This was my first glimpse of the boss. He was as I expected, a tough guy with a menacing frown and a gritty voice. Walking into the garden felt a bit awkward. I walked in and was met at the corner of the building by the boss. His name was Steve McGrath. I was expecting a formal interview, but this was nothing like I expected. I'd gone along with my leather portfolio with my certificates and my CV enclosed. How naive was I. This wasn't 'an interview' this was a 'sizing up'. I was told that if I wanted work I needed to supply and wear black trousers with a black bomber jacket. The pub he was going to put me at had staff t-shirts, which I'd be expected to wear. He spoke briefly advising me to take out a workplace injury insurance policy. The piece of paper this was on was a photocopy and had no credibility to me, so I declined. He pointed out I could get thousands of pounds for a broken nose or broken fingers and any other injuries listed that he started to rattle off. I wasn't interested. He was talking about taking money out of the wages for the cover and he'd sort it all out. I didn't feel comfortable with any of this and thought to myself, I have to supply clothing, I was being encouraged to pay insurance, it just seemed like I would be paying out before I could earn anything. He went on to say he'd book me in for restraint training, which in Southampton was conducted by the Police. The Police were beginning to introduce the door-licensing scheme.

'Can you start this Thursday?' he asked.

'Sure, no problem.'

I'd begun having mixed feelings about this, excitement that he'd offered me a position, but on the other hand, what had I got myself into? I sensed that this company seemed a bit of a rough set-up and my Church life background and voluntary organisation work experience wasn't going to prepare me for any of this. I'd had near scrapes but had never really been in a punch up ever before. School days excluded. I had a couple of occurrences in my school life where punches flew, but these were merely taps and no broken noses ever occurred. I grew up with the Christian youth crowd, so my life experiences had been pretty safe.

It came to Thursday, and I was getting myself ready for the evening. I had a set of clippers to do my own hair, so in preparation for the first shift the hair was off with a grade one trim. It's almost the stereotypical view of a bouncer. Grade one haircut, all in black with a bomber jacket. I turned up at the pub called Sally's Café Bar. It was a safe start and I felt happy with that.

The manager was a young female called Becky. She was a very glamorous twenty-something. She was cute, but she was the boss, and you could tell that straight away. All I wanted to do was please her, do my job well and keep her and her pub safe. She walked me around the building. The downstairs was split into two sections the cafe and the bar. At night the cafe would be closed. She then showed me upstairs, where there was the cocktail bar. All chrome and neon lights, this was a very trendy bar, a popular bar for the student population.

Her assistant manager was Ray. He was of black Caribbean descent, fit, and muscular yet absolutely useless behind the bar. Becky often used to give him funny looks, for things he'd say to her that sounded a bit flirty. I found out from her that he was new and taking ages to find his feet. He's slow and preferred to chat to punters than actually get some work done. He was to be my first line of backup when he was around ... great. I hoped he'd at least be reliable in that department. I found out from Becky that the owner of the pub visited regularly and he expected me to be on the door constantly, meeting and greeting the punters, not letting the riff-raff in and dealing with trouble when it arose. She told me the staff t-shirts were an important part of the company image and these had to be ironed and clean for every shift. I knew this shouldn't be too difficult.

Becky had a radio to call me if there was any concern inside the bar. This was the first moment I found out I was to be a lone worker. I had a radio in contact with another local pub for Pro-Security backup in emergencies only, but they were minutes away. I came to a quick understanding that by the time they got to a car and drove over, it would take them five minutes or so, and for me, that'd be five minutes or so too late. I'll be honest and say I was slightly nervous about this thought. There were two doors into the pub and even though one was an exit only, this posed a potential problem where people could let someone in who wasn't supposed to be there. With only one doorman, I saw this as an issue straight away.

It was 7pm, my first shift had started and I was out on the door. The students were beginning to turn up. I was being polite and courteous, opening doors for people entering and exiting the premises. One person commented saying how nice I was, realising I was new to the job. Deep down, if something kicked off, I didn't know if I could cope with it. My boss Steve turned up. He briefly spoke to me on the door, asked if everything was alright, then walked on in. As I looked though the glass door, I could see Steve talking to Becky. He didn't stop long, probably twenty minutes.

As he left he said 'Becky's happy with you and said you're doing ok. Are you alright for three nights a week, Thursday, Friday and Saturday, 7 to 12?'

I couldn't say no. He was offering me more hours and Becky was apparently happy with me.

Later on that night, a bloke came to the door, introduced himself and started chatting to me about door work. He seemed a bit of a know it all, you know the sort, the type that you'd rather walk away from instead of have a pointless conversation with. I didn't want to let him know too much about me so I closed up a bit. He asked me the company I worked for. I told him it was Pro-Security. He looked a tad shocked.

'How long have you worked for them?'

I replied that I had just started.

'You know you're working for the McGrath Brothers right? You don't want to upset them.'

It was a case of acting up. I felt the need to portray that I was no walk over and I was one of Steve's men.

With that I shrugged my shoulders and said, 'So what, are you going in or not?' again trying to close off the conversation. I didn't want to appear concerned by what he had said or what he was implying. He eventually went on in and I stood at the door pondering on the thoughts in my head about who the person was that I actually worked for? What had I got myself into?

Although this was a trouble free night, it was an eye-opener into the nightlife from the view of a doorman. I knew the day of trouble was to come but for now, it felt good.

'SEE YOU ON
THE STREETS
LADS'

'SEE YOU ON THE STREETS LADS'

02

When people found out what I did for a living they used to ask...
'Was it rough?' and probably more often than not this was followed
up with 'Did you ever get hurt?' It wasn't a glamorous job but
people used to express an interest in what stories I had to tell. I
was a member of staff for a pub/nightclub security group. To
elaborate, I was a 'doorman' for the pubs and clubs, or put simply
a 'Bouncer'

I'd had my introduction and now it was time for the training.
At the start of the two-day training I took myself along to the local
police station. The police obviously had an interest in who was
working the doors. I knew that this experience was a two-fold
exercise. They wanted to know us and train us. We couldn't work
the doors without their license to do so. It was a requirement for
employment in Southampton pubs and clubs. The Government
introduced a licensing scheme but this didn't officially start until
2001. Southampton Council was ahead of the game, acting as
pilots or initiators for the Security Industries Act (SIA) Licensing
Scheme. The focus on the first day was classroom learning. They

covered the functions of door security personnel and what the expected behaviour was, including customer care skills. They introduced the topic of conflict management and how to deal with difficult customers. They took us through the safety aspects of body searching people and what to do in emergencies. They also told us that we were responsible for preventing over crowding and we were the ones who would be fined for letting people into the premises over the number allowed. We were told that a doorman could be fined up to £10,000 for failure to keep within the legal capacity. When I heard this I asked Steve whether he supplied number clickers, you'll know the answer already. I went out and bought a number clicker and still have it to this day. This day ended with a multiple-choice exam. If you'd listened to the training sessions the exam was not too difficult.

The second day came and this was the physical restraint training. I had done similar training before when working with adults with learning difficulties. But this seemed more real life. I knew I was going to be using this training. This training was about self-defence and has stuck with me, even after 10 years. I don't want to go into what was trained in detail, but I had confidence in what I had learnt and now had the necessary training to handle most situations. I knew how to protect myself from the use of weapons and being struck by violent individuals. I remember the guy who I was partnered up with for the training. He looked hard as nails. But when it came to the role playing and practising, he wasn't as strong as he looked. He'd get me in an arm lock and tweak for the pain, but I felt nothing. I pulled out of the hold really easily. I told him to try again but this time, get me to tap out. I tried to push it a little for a bit of realism. He eventually got me locked but he did struggle, claiming he didn't want to hurt me. When the roles reversed, I had either over compensated on strength or he wasn't cut out for this type of work. I locked him up very easily forcing him to tap quickly. His pain barrier was set very low, I almost felt sorry for him.

After the training we all sat down and the trainers reported back with the previous days' exam results, handed out the licenses and thanked us for taking part. The trainer wished us well and said the memorable words 'See you on the streets lads.'

I wondered about the need for the licensing in Southampton and wondered if it was because of the boss and his reputation. Whether it was because the police wanted to know more about who worked for people like him and their backgrounds. They claimed the purpose of the training was about integrating the security industry with the police to form a stronger force against crime and violence. However, the root cause for this we all know is about getting rid of the rogue firms who used to sort out the punters either by battering them, throwing them through doors or down stairways. Since the SIA's introduction you have to agree, the reputation of the doorman has improved from the 1980's and 1990's.

Steve McGrath had a reputation as being a tough guy. The best way to describe him is that he was like one of the Mitchell brothers, he looked like Phil Mitchell from Eastenders, that dismal London based TV soap drama. He wouldn't thank me for that, but I'm sure it's not the first time. His brother Pete was rarely seen out and about, but his reputation was worse than Steve's. They were known as 'the McGrath Brothers'. When anyone tells you they're known as The 'So and So' Brothers, it's never a good sign. When he walked around he had three or four guys with him. They were usually suited and were always close to him. These guys weren't just mates, they were paid protection.

It didn't take long for the action to start in Sally's Café Bar. I was stood at the door when I heard the radio voice of Becky in a panic. I ran in and looked towards the bar. Ray was there looking blank at me, as if to say 'what's up?'

'Where's Becky?' I shouted over the music.

He shrugged his shoulders.

With that I started to run up the stairs. I saw out of the corner of my eye that Ray began to move and follow me. I got upstairs and two people were arguing with aggression in their eyes. It was at the point of no return, the argument could settle or explode. I walked straight in and made a quick assessment as to who was the aggressor. Standing between them I looked and shouted at the aggressor. 'Times up mate, you're leaving right now! Either by walking or me helping you, you choose?'

The man began shouting around me at the other person, so I eyeballed him putting my face up close to his and firmly said 'Now! You choose?' The man turned, shouting threats at the other person. I left Ray upstairs with the guy the aggressor had been arguing with. As I walked by him to go downstairs I said 'Keep them in here and start finding out what happened'. I walked down the stairs following the aggressor and escorted him off the premises. At the door, I told him to move away from the pub entrance and fight his battles somewhere else. He wanted the other man to fight with. I told him that the guy would not be leaving until he had left the area. For his safety I would keep him inside till he had gone. His anger then became directed at me. I firmly stood my ground, again eyeballing him up close to his face.

'Go for it, and see how far you get!'

The man backed down and began walking backwards onto the street, shouting towards the upstairs window. When he was out of sight I walked back in. Becky wanted the other man to leave too. So I walked up to him and said unfortunately it was his turn next. He was worried the other chap would be outside. I told him the guy had left the area, but he had to leave now. When I got him to the door, I told him where the other guy went so that he could go in the opposite direction. When he'd gone I went back in to speak to Becky and Ray. I confirmed with Becky that it was all dealt with, asked if she was ok, then thanked Ray for his help. Once I'd got the all clear I went back on the door to carry on with the night. But the truth of it all, I was shaking with adrenaline. My knees were rattling with fear of the 'what ifs?' What if it got rough? What if he hit me? What if I had to get him out physically? What if? What if? What if? I was starting to worry about the day I'd actually have to use my training for the first time. At the end of the shift I touched base with Becky, who appeared happy with the way it was dealt with, which encouraged me in to thinking I did ok. Despite the what-ifs, I was beginning to get a taste for this.

The next night, Steve made his usual Saturday night check-up visit. Having spent the day thinking about the night before, I began to think more and more about how I'd like a second guy to help out. We had two doors to the pub and one man couldn't watch both. He said I didn't need one. I wasn't happy with this but felt I couldn't do much about it. Without me knowing he'd already spoken to Becky about this, expressing my concern, and they'd agreed I could have a second person on Saturdays only.

The following week I had a partner, someone I could work with. I haven't a clue what his real name was, he introduced himself as 'Rocky' and that's what stuck. He was an amateur boxer, slim, bald and about 20 years old. He was a good lad, fast and feisty. He stood at the bottom of the stairs keeping an eye on the other door from the inside, about three or four metres from the main entrance. On his first night, he slung some geezer through the door. With the guy outside, Rocky said to me, 'He's done, barred, don't ever let him back in!'

The bewildered man who hadn't even realised he'd been chucked out until he'd turned around and realised he was outside.

'What was that for?' he said.

I had to agree with him, I had no clue as to why he was chucked out, but I had to deal with this on the door.

'You tell me?' I said.

He genuinely had no clue. Nothing he would tell me anyway.

'Well my colleague says you're barred, so I guess you won't be back here again, so find yourself another place to drink, goodnight.'

With that I walked back in to the bar to speak to Rocky about what had happened. The guy left the entrance and walked away having no-one to talk to. Rocky started to tell me that he was being a nuisance with the girls in the bar and Becky said he had to leave. Rocky had manhandled a guy who didn't even know he would be leaving.

Rocky had an, 'act now, think later' approach. On occasions this caused more problems than necessary. As the weeks went by, I was finding that when I was on my own we had very few problems, but now having Rocky about, all someone had to do was sneeze and he'd be on 'em. Up until now, we got to choose who we kicked out. Although with Rocky sometimes I wasn't included in the decision-making, but most of the time we communicated and agreed a drunken student had crossed the line and needed to find somewhere else to drink that night.

One Saturday, we had a major kick off, two guys decided to give it some, grabbing each other by their clothing they were swinging themselves around the seating area, knocking tables and chairs over. The glasses were smashing on to the floor and Becky was shouting at Rocky and I to get it sorted. She knew she'd have to end up paying for the damage. As we got to the top of the stairs it looked a war zone. It was messy. Rocky dived in with no fear onto one of the guys, I had to deal with the other. I thought 'this is it, this is what the training was for'.

The guy continued to grab hold of his opponent even when Rocky had him in a bear hug, picking the lad off his feet. All I had to do was lock my one down and get him outside. I moved in. As I did, I grabbed hold of the lad's arm. As I twisted it the guy struggled. He got out of the hold and the take down got messy, arms flying everywhere. I struggled with this guy, but he was nothing, he was a scrawny late teens student, what did I do wrong? I knew what it was. I was scared.

Most people who left usually didn't need much persuasion and ended up outside. This was my first tough case. The problem was not that I'd forgotten the training, but the nerves affected my strength. I vowed that this would never happen again, for my own safety and a less embarrassing take down. I was supposed to be the doorman and my reputation counted on being able to take guys down when needed. I had to shake off the fear, I knew I could do the job, I just had to apply the strength and be hard as nails when I needed to be.

We used to get paid cash for our work. I never knew how kosher this was, but didn't ask questions. It was regular so I didn't want to end up being a nuisance with the boss.

At the end of the night Rocky turned to me and said 'I'm going over the road are you coming for a drink?' This was unusual. Normally his girlfriend picked him up, I'd go to my car and we both went off home. I thought ah' what the heck.

'Sounds like a good idea, let's get a pint.'

Over the road was a dingy looking club with a purple neon sign. The club was called 'Flava Lounge'. It was a dark street and the building looked rough. It had big bouncers on the door, and usually a queue of people for most of the time. As people left, they'd let in the next in the queue. As we approached the club, I headed for the back of the queue, but Rocky walked on, he looked back at me and smiled, and with a little laugh said 'We don't need to queue, come on.'

The guys on the door stepped to one side, greeted us with handshakes and we walked in. Hang on a second this doorman lark was getting me into clubs. I didn't even know these guys, but they let me in.

'Do they work for Steve?' I asked Rocky

'No, some other firm, they know me, I'm a regular.' He turned away to look at some girl, turned back to me and continued, 'They know you, I've told 'em you're alright.'

The music was loud, it was drum and bass and the crowd were all dancing. This was a true dance club. The bar was long and the bar staff were in abundance handing over the drinks to the punters. It was an open space with a bricked wall interior and black metal old style staircases. Lights flashing and the smoke machine working overtime, the atmosphere felt good, the music was so loud you couldn't even hear yourself think, although you couldn't stop yourself from starting to foot tap to the beat. I stood back against the bar and began looking for the security. There were three guys inside and two on the door. One was stood at the balcony looking over the dance floor. Another was halfway down the stairs and the third was stood close to the DJ.

As I stood by the bar the crowd looked like they were preoccupied with all the dancing and socializing. I, however, felt detached from this, and just felt like this was an extension of the shift, keeping one eye on the dance floor for trouble and the other on the doorman to see what they were up to. These guys were using sleeve-clipped microphones, all of them. They had total communication with the guys on the door, the entire security team inside and the bar staff. They looked organised, they looked big and they looked like they meant business.

It was the first Friday in December 1997, and Steve came along to the Sally's Café Bar. I usually worked on my own on Fridays but Rocky was there. I didn't know why he was there, Rocky usually only worked Saturdays, but when I saw Steve, I thought the worst. I was about to get the boot for not being good enough or not being tough enough for the job. Steve came over to me, looked me in the eyes, and told Rocky to go inside. Rocky gave me a look as if to say good luck and went on inside.

'Is everything ok Steve?' I asked.

'Everything's good Neil, everything's good,' he replied, 'I want you to do something for me' he started.

At this point I almost breathed a sigh of relief, but I wasn't quite sure what he wanted me to do.

'I've got a new venue and I want you to be the doorman there.'

'HAVE
ANOTHER
GO AND
SEE HOW FAR
YOU GET!'

'HAVE ANOTHER GO AND SEE HOW FAR YOU GET!'

03

If you asked a member of public 'What would the common doorman wear?' The bomber jacket is what they may say. Part of the bouncer image of the nineties was the black bomber jacket. This was our protection from the cold nights when stood on the doors. It was the type MA1 and was specifically sealed from the cold air with a zippered pocket on the sleeve with 2 pencil slots. I was probably the only one to actually have a pen in a slot and a small notepad in the zipped pocket. I always thought it'd be useful one day, but I kept on losing the pen.

Changing the subject, here's a useless fact. My childhood hero B.A. 'I pity the fool' Baracus from The A Team, actor Mr T, real name Laurence Tureaud, was a bouncer in his early years before his acting career. In the typical American way of having competitions for everything, they had the National Toughest Bouncer Competitions which Mr T won twice. Funny how Americans will have a competition for anything. He'd probably win 'the most milk drunk in a TV series award' too. Oh sweet memories. Memories of jeeps blowing up and the men getting up and dusting themselves off.

It's a common misconception that the main requirement for a bouncer is being a tough guy. It's more than that, it's about communication skills and intellect. Being able to assess a situation and work out the best course of action in a short amount of time, with the least amount of fuss was vitally important. No bar manager wants too much fuss or distraction that can affect the reputation or atmosphere of the pub or club.

This is probably the quality that Steve saw in me. It wasn't that I was your typical tough guy, it was more than likely the professional attitude that I had for the job. I took the job seriously. Every time I went on shift I'd check for first aid kits, fire extinguishers and ensure fire exits were clear. I was good at my job, but didn't realise how good at the time. I thought Steve wanted a tough guy, until that day when he said the words, 'I've got a new venue and I want you to be the doorman there'.

Rocky was told to do more hours at Sally's Café Bar, hence why he was there that night. He didn't know what was said to me until I explained afterwards. He was a bit annoyed with Steve for getting him in to work on his own. He didn't like the idea of lone-working, and said he reckoned he'd leave because he didn't want Steve to expect this of him. Becky wasn't too pleased about this either. We'd built up a relationship of trust, we knew how each other worked and what was allowable or not. She was happy with the way I would talk to customers and deal with situations without making too much fuss. In a way, I was sad to move on too, I liked the bunch that worked there.

However, when Steve told me I was moving to a new venue, I felt happy that I'd obviously proved I could do the job, especially as it would be a new venue for him. I had earned trust from him to do the job and do it well. He was leaving Rocky at Sally's Café Bar, and I was off to the dockside pub restaurant, 'Los Barcos Restaurante'.

It was a Spanish themed pub on the dockside. It had lots of wood for décor and boat paraphernalia around, like ships wheels, oars, sails and had dusty pewter tankards hanging over the bar. It had a restaurant at one end where food would be served and at the other end a dance floor, big enough for about a dozen people. Any more than this and the dance floor would be a bit of a squeeze.

On my first night, I had a chance to have a good look around and see the entrances in and out of the bar. At the back of the bar was a shopping precinct entrance that would close at 6pm. At the restaurant end of the venue we had another entrance. Then there was the main entrance for the bar, which opened on to the dockside. Steve told me that I'd be working with one other chap on the door and there would be a guy inside keeping an eye on things. I was told I needed to be on the main door at all times. Although without earpieces, we each had a radio, which would help our communications. These weren't supplied by Pro-Security but by the pub themselves. Looking around I saw a potential problem area, the corridor to the toilets. This was completely out of site to security, so I made it part of the routine check up, to walk through the corridor and check on the male and female toilets. For the female toilets we'd ask a lady leaving the loo if all was ok in there. Most would politely reply informing us all was ok, some took this as a bit of fun and encouraged us to check it out ourselves and other banter. The gents' loo, we could check. This would be every 15-20 minutes. At the end of the corridor, you'd come to the restaurant area.

The clientele had changed too from the previous bar. It's no longer the young students, these were the town folk, known as the townies. These usually attracted more grief with the door staff and would test my patience to the limits. The townies and the students were never a good mix. The first night went off without a hitch. The first couple of weeks I was taking time to get used to the punters and they were getting used to me. Los Barcos was a real eye opener, it was rougher and louder and I had to maintain Steve's personal and business reputation.

This venue was more prone to kick-offs than Sallys Café Bar. One Friday night, I walked in and picked up the radios from behind the bar. The barman came over and pointed me to a group of lads who had been sat there all afternoon. They'd already had a warning for their loud behaviour. Because it was early, there were still families in the restaurant area. These guys appeared well gone, something I wish they were, 'gone'. I walked over to them to make myself known and to let them know I was aware they'd had their warnings and not to push it or they'd be leaving. They respected that and said they'd keep it down. The other security guys turned up. Ahmed, a turban wearing Asian, he was thin and short and very difficult to understand with his strong accent. Nice guy but a slow thinker. The other guy was Dom. He was the one with me on the door. He was a white male, again thin and short. He looked like he'd had some army training. However, he was a boaster, he'd boast about anything. His car was better than mine, his shoes were the best, his missus was the best and his experience was the best. He was a total nuisance. Ahmed on the other hand worked inside. I never found out much about him. One thing I knew about him was that he'd never call us for any bother on the inside. The reason for this was he was a total plank, oblivious to anything going on. We'd get our calls from the bar staff. Whenever it did kick-off he was never there. He'd go to cover the door while Dom and I went in to deal with stuff. Ahmed wasn't told to go to the door, but that's what he did. When we'd get back there after having dealt with something, he'd say, 'Where did you guys go?' The bar wasn't a huge venue. If he'd opened his eyes he would have seen us. I got the distinct impression he avoided the trouble.

Anyway, the loud lads got louder and louder, and the bar staff called me to get them to leave, they'd had enough. I walked up to them, and the verbal abuse started. Once the guys stood up from their seats Dom and I took the main geezers by the arm and walked them to the door. Their cronies walked on behind and left with them. When we got outside they continued to hurl abuse. The question on this occasion was, where's Ahmed? He came to the main entrance shortly after.

'Is everything ok? I notice those guys have gone?'

Ahmed would not be working with me for much longer as I was on the phone to Steve. He'd been on the loo. This wasn't the first time this loo excuse occurred, it happened about three or four times when he should have been lending a hand. Because there were too many of the guys for Dom and I to really deal with, his help would have been most useful on this occasion. He had a radio, so why didn't he hear my call. He said he didn't get the message. I'm sorry, this was utter tosh and he had to go. Steve moved him on by the following night. He had lasted about 4 weeks. Dom in his own way was just as useless. I had established my own high standards and Dom grated with me somewhat. His attitude towards customers stank. He'd be cocky and sarky with folks, which for me never sat comfortably. I wanted our guys to be nice 100% of the time. Good customer relations were important to me. It was this reputation that solved problems much quicker. When it was time to lay hands on people I wanted it done quickly, firmly and with the minimal of disruption to the atmosphere in the pub.

The following night a guy decided to accept the challenge to swim to the nearest jetty. Outside the bar, Los Barcos had a railing close by towards the water's edge, where some boats were moored. His friends were cheering him on. I could see the backs of heads looking out into the water. I walked over to the railing and there was this guy swimming. Well it was less swimming and more bobbing. His head was starting to go under, this guy was struggling. I radioed the bar staff to call the marina guards to attend. Some panicking women shouted at me to jump in and rescue him. I made it quite clear I couldn't do that because he was too far out. It was also a ten-foot drop to the water. The shock of this and the cold would be enough to take it out of anyone. If he was struggling, then most likely so would I. Within minutes the marine guards came by in their patrol boat. Shining their bright torch light around the water, they found the guy and pulled him onboard. They bundled him into an ambulance and sent him off to the City Hospital. This guy would have a surprise bit of mail within the next few days from the marine guards with an invoice for his rescue, due to his unnecessary stupid behaviour. He was going to be charged around fifty quid for their trouble.

I'd noticed over time that it wasn't the men we got the most grief from but the women. The one that had shouted at me to go into the water wouldn't let up, accusing me of negligence. I must have repeated myself half a dozen times, saying to her, 'It's not my duty to rescue the guy from the water... I am not trained for life guarding.' If she had a problem with this, she could speak to the marine guards or the police. I was satisfied that this was not my problem, but I think we could put this down to her drunken behaviour.

Depending on what the night was like, depended on whether it was a curry night. With the harassing woman on my case, this was definitely a curry night. On my way home I drove to my usual, parked up outside and tooted the car horn. I looked over at the window, the curtain pulled back and the thumbs up signal appeared. It was my regular order from the usual take out. What was even better was the waiters would bring it to the car for me. The usual cost for the eight quid forty meal of chicken biryani and a keema naan was just a fiver for me. It was a nice discount or perk of the job. When I went home, I told my fellow housemates what had happened with our friend who'd gone off to hospital. With more crazy events like this and more hands on action, the nighttime reports were getting more interesting.

It was a warm Saturday in April 1998, and I'd been at El Barcos now for about three and half months. My confidence was well established and I had a zero tolerance approach to hassle. Dom and Ahmed were long gone, but I still found that Steve was using the venue for young inexperienced door supervisors. I was working with a geezer called Richard. I called him Rich, but you get to call him Mr Edwards... Nah, just kidding. He was just as useless as Dom. But the conversation was better and when you spent many hours on the door with someone, common interests were helpful for conversation. Ahmed's replacement for the inside lasted about a month and we hadn't seen anyone since. So it's just Rich and I working there.

Stood at the door welcoming people in, we got a radio call from the bar staff saying it was kicking off by the restaurant. Ok, picture this, on a Friday or Saturday night things got a little busy, but on that night we were crammed. The bar area was five rows of people thick and there was no way to walk through them, not without wasting valuable time. Behind those people was a long table running the length of the bar counter. At this table there were seats both sides and each chair was occupied by a group celebrating some workplace occasion. It seemed like a busy, happy, trouble free night till this radio call. Rich and I turned opening both doors to the pub and walked in. Seeing the crowd, I stood up on an empty seat to see where the trouble was. Usually whenever anyone says 'There's trouble in here', it's usually just a bit of pushing and shoving and plenty of verbal. What I witnessed was a full-on boxing match at the end of the long table. We needed to get in and fast. I turned to Rich, and said, 'Follow me'.

With that I'd left the seat and walked the length of the table. People hurriedly reached for their glasses and bottles of wine, clearing the way for me to jump off the end in-between the two fighters. Holding them apart I turned back to my colleague, who looked in a state of shock, still standing by the main door. I had jumped into a situation without backup because Rich didn't follow me. With that he saw the look in my eyes and began squeezing passed people by the bar. When he got there I firmly said to him 'This man is leaving via the restaurant'.

Once Rich had the guys arm, I released my grip on the front of his shirt. Still having a hold on the other guy I pushed him towards the nearest wall, turned him around so his back was towards me and pulled his arm up his back. Once Rich came back we took the tougher of the two fighters out together. This guy was struggling and by the time we got him to the door his buddies were coming to chip in. We seemed to be getting a fair bit of grief for our troubles. Once we were outside I told Rich to go back in. With that I turned to the guys who were all becoming quite verbal and said, 'Enough is enough gents, anyone who fights leaves and anyone who doesn't like that leaves too, you guys are not welcome here again, please find somewhere else to drink.'

With that said, I walked back in leaving them outside. Looking outside through the glass doors, the guys lingered about for a short time getting our casual glances and shouting obscenities towards us.

Eventually, without gaining a reaction from us, they moved on. I turned to Rich, placed my hand on his shoulder, eyeballing him and said 'Next time I say to follow me, I mean follow me, even if that means walking on tables'. He smirked and shook his head at me. I think he thought I was a bit of a nutter. This was Rich's first major kick off. Rich handled his guy fine and got stuck in when needed. Even though he didn't walk on tables, he was ok.

Most of the time, we got a hassle free night, but as the warmer weather started coming, something in the atmosphere was changing the way people acted. It was another warm night and the sun setting glow was giving off a golden colour across the waterside. Inside the pub, the bar staff were just changing over from restaurant to pub staff. The restaurant was clearing up and the families were beginning to leave. It was a couple of hours into the shift and we got a call from the bar manager about some rowdy lads who they wanted to leave the premises. Rich and I walked in and stood inside by the main doors to identify the guys. The bar manager pointed them out via the radio, counting the number of tables away. Once I'd seen the guys, I told Rich to wait by the door while I went in and asked them to leave quietly.

I walked over to the chaps full of my usual confidence, expecting a positive response. I asked the lad who appeared to be the ringleader for a quiet word away from the others. As I walked back towards the main entrance, I realised the bloke hadn't followed me. What is it with people not wanting to follow me? I walked back over.

'Excuse me, I don't think I made myself clear when I asked you to pop over there for a quiet chat, as you didn't come over. You need to know I have been asked to come over and ask you guys to leave, so if you wouldn't mind, rather than making a fuss of it all, just finish your drinks and make a move.'

This didn't go to plan. The guys laughed this off. I eyeballed Rich and he promptly came over. I leaned in and said to the main character.

'I've never got to the point where I ask a third time, now you've tried my patience. Last chance to do this nicely, I need you guys to get up and make your way to the door and move on.'

With this, the guy who was sat at the table with his mates, turned towards me looking up, pointed his arm at me and said 'I ain't going anywhere pal, you want me to go, make me.'

As soon as he said this, before he realised what had happened, glasses smashed as they hit the floor and the drinks were spilt across the table. I had grabbed his arm and twisted it, using my strength and weight I'd pressed his shoulder into the table. His face hitting the table, I used my arm to hold his head on the table. He didn't have the strength to move out of this hold. I moved my face into his, nice and close.

'Maybe I didn't make myself clear, I'm telling you now how we are going to do this... we're going to be leaving, got it?'

He acknowledged this and appeared to oblige. I think I'd got his attention. Rich was concentrating on his mates and watching my back. Next I said to him 'k, we're going to walk to the exit nice and slow and you're now leaving. Right?'

He replied with a simple, 'Ok.'

Keeping hold of his arm, I pulled him away from the table. Using a wrist hold I tweaked his arm for sharp instalments of pain, to let him know I had control of this and expected him to comply. After getting him outside, I walked back in and offered his mates the same treatment, or they could walk out now with the minimal of fuss. They surprisingly walked with no hassle. Once they were all out, Rich and I stood by the door. The main man began to act up now he was outside, so I turned to Rich and said, 'Lets go inside, there's no need to listen to this act rattle on.'

As Rich turned to go inside, I was just turning myself and I saw out of the corner of my eye, a plastic chair flying in towards Rich's head. I put my arm above his head and took the full impact on my arm. I span the chair over and with the legs pointing towards the attacker I wrapped the legs of the chair around his body. Pushing the chair against him I was able to move him where I wanted him. I moved him towards the nearest wall and rammed the chair so hard the legs snapped and the seat section slammed into his chest, knocking the wind out of him. It was the guy I'd escorted out. He wasn't letting up.

'Have another go and see how far you get!' I shouted up close to his face.

Rich came over and said with a smile, 'What happened?'

'He was only about to wrap this chair round your head, literally inches from your head Rich!'

With that Rich replied, 'Oh did he?' and then kicked him hard in the shin. Rich wore steel toecaps for exactly this purpose.

The man crumpled in pain as I released the chair from his chest. He grabbed his shin on his left leg. With that, I turned to Rich and said 'Inside now!' I turned to the guy and said, 'Enough of this, now clear off and don't come back.'

The guy stood up and said, 'You don't know who I am, I'll be back to have ya'. He raised his arms pointing his fingers at me as if they were pistols, 'Bang Bang... watch your back guys, I'm coming back to sort you two out!'

'DON'T WORRY THE BLOODS NOT MINE'

04

Patience was a necessity for this job. Times had changed and bar managers wanted a professional image, but they wanted to know that the doorman could handle situations if required to. Don't get me wrong, I'm a patient guy, or at least I thought I was. After a year of doing this I was beginning to gain more and more confidence and if anyone tried my patience I was finding I'd snap quicker than before and I took no messing.

The role of the bouncer was to be the front liners for the police. They'd often turn up once we had everything under control, to check that all was ok. The CCTV cameras turned to face pub entrances and that's just the start of it. You can imagine the CCTV operator now, sat there with a cracking cuppa and some bourbon creams saying over the police radio, 'Hang on there chaps, the door supervisors are trying to get the crowd under control, they seem to be doing ok… one door supervisor has a man detained and ready… you can move in now officers, the door supervisors have the situation safe.' On one occasion I remember seeing the van pull up at a distance, waiting for us to have the situation under control. They then moved in, arrested the restrained punter, putting them into the police van and off they went. They had left us to do our job and they came in to do theirs. We were the frontline for them to come along and pick them up.

Thankfully the threats of repercussions were empty threats and I never saw any violent backlashes. But at the time you can't help yourself but be a little cautious. I often wondered what my car would look like at the end of my shift, or if they'd be waiting in the car park for me. This last threat, to come back with guns, did worry me at the time and I was watching my back fearing it could happen at any time. The sooner I got out of this venue the better. Almost on cue, Steve phoned me one afternoon to ask me to go and clean up a venue for him.

It was a new venue, but it'd had recent trouble with a useless security firm, who made a pig's ear of things. Steve told me to go and sort it out, set up the standards and when it was all settled, hand it on to some newbies to take over. He told me the location, the times and that was that. I got no choice in the matter and I was now finding that he was moving me around venues too often and there was no stability in income. What may have been four nights was now turning into three or even sometimes two nights. It wasn't the work that was a problem, I enjoyed working all over the place, what I needed was the money. I needed a fair whack each week to pay rent and bills whilst doing this study thing.

This new venue was an Irish bar. This was a major change in punters compared to the last two. The music was different and we weren't in a student part of town. This was a much older bunch of hardened drinkers, with a reputation for kicking off regularly.

This pub didn't have a drug problem or a binge drinking problem, it was just aggro. You only had to look at a guy to get his back up. The owners were new and they wanted a nicer welcome than the one they had received. The main problem was one particular bunch of blokes who thought they had every right to walk behind the bar, help themselves to drinks and put it on a tab they had with the previous owners. The owners spoke to us about this and said that any objection to this usually aroused foul language and disrupted other punters in the bar area. The landlord continued by saying 'The last firm we had in couldn't handle it, didn't turn up one evening and left us stranded. The thing is this, we want them barred and we want them out.'

I clearly understood what they were asking of me and said to the landlord and his wife that it'd need more than two of us to deal with this and that I'd speak to Steve and arrange for backup one evening next week to deal with it. We couldn't deal with this on our own, that'd be daft. I might look the part, but the potential of a full on brawl, needed backup. What I wanted to do was lead them into a false sense of security, pardon the pun. I knew we could deal with this, but I wanted to do the job quick and fast without them realising what happened.

For the next few nights, I watched them with interest, sussing out who's who. Who could be the potential problem and who were the spectators of the group? I learned more about the venue and where we could exit them, rather than the main doors and where there was CCTV cover. The CCTV systems were a blessing for us in one sense meaning that court evidence was useful to put individuals inside. But, what about the doorman who gets involved, the cameras record everything. It's normal for any doorman to take a mental of note of where the cameras are and where the blind spots are too. After assessing who were the main problems and who were the followers of the group, I worked out we had five to deal with. Two were real potential for problems. The other three were not so much of a concern. I thought they'd walk with a bit of help.

During the next week I was constantly thinking about the likely kick off we were going to have on Thursday, trying to get these guys out. I had phoned Steve, who agreed to send us a team of four extra guys for the job. We needed to do this on Thursday, so as not to ruin a good Friday or Saturday night. Steve mentioned he might pop in at some point, to show his face around, intending to let people know who our boss was. His reputation as being a hard man in the town was well known by many. This should send them a clear message that something was up.

Thursday was here and my day of studies was somewhat non-existent. I had sat through the lectures throughout the day wondering how the evening was going to work out. My mind was a little pre-occupied with the thought of agro. My appetite suffered, and for those that know me, you'd agree, this is really unusual and shows my feeling of worry about how the evening would work out. The plan was this. My colleague and I would turn up as usual. Using a radio, we'd be in contact with our back up who would be sat in the car out of sight around the corner. We were to radio them when we were happy that the ringleader was in and the others were there. We didn't want to deal with just one of them. We wanted all of them there. One individual at a time wouldn't have the same impact of force. We wanted the force element to send them the message they were no longer welcome.

Stood on the door, the individuals started to arrive. All appeared like a normal night in their world. I was feeling a little anxious about how this was all going to go off. The time was about 8:15pm, and the group had been in for about half an hour. The landlord was constantly looking over to us at the door. He was being a bit of a nuisance to us in that you could see something wasn't right. I checked on the radio with the backup, whether they were ready to do this 'Ready when you are Neil', a slight pause on the radio and the second message came through from another backup chap.

'Come on what are we waiting for?'

It seemed as though these guys were ready for anything. Ready to deliver a message.

I think back at this and think I'd hired in heavies to deal with a problem. I had enough clout with the boss to request heavies. Never before had I ordered a job like this. What was I doing?

'Let's do it then lads!' I called on the radio.

Within seconds the car pulled up over the road, the doors opened, the guys got out and started walking over.

This was the muscle. You could see in the eyes of these guys, they meant business. This was Steve's personal collection for these kinds of jobs. I turned to go in and began to walk over to the corner where the chaps were sat. I walked over to our ringleader.

'Hiya Brian, sorry to have to do this, but I need to say to you and your friends you're all barred and I expect you now to leave.' He hadn't noticed the backup by the door, so just laughed this off. Some laughed with him, and began heckling.

'Let's see him kick us all out'.

Some others looked puzzled and couldn't believe what was just said to them.

Two chaps could see the backup and pointed over at the door telling Brian to turn around. Brian looked over his shoulder at the main entrance, then looked back at me and said 'Why did you bring the boys in, couldn't you handle it yourself?'

As he stood up, he brought his hands towards me to grab my shirt. I thought to myself, this is it! It's built up to this moment. As he laid his hands on me, the chair legs scraped on the floor, his guys began getting out of their seats and our guys moved in. I don't recall much of the detail. It was a commotion for a minute or so. Punches were being exchanged and the other blokes were putting up a fight.

As for me, I was trained to restrain not fight. I had Brian by the arm and rotated it beautifully. He put up a struggle and it wasn't long before my colleague came in to assist. I grabbed his right arm, with my colleague on his left. This guy was strong. I couldn't handle this guy on my own, even with the colleague on the other side. In my view the only option was to get him on the floor. When I had my balance and the opportunity, I rammed my foot into the back of his knee. He crumpled to the floor, slamming his knee down onto the hard wooden floor. At this point I had to put all my strength in to the arm to force his body into the ground. Once we got him there, I held on to him as tight as I could. Looking around the room, it was like a scene out of an old western. A chair was up in the air about to be wrapped around someone's head. Scuffle huddles were dotted around and gradually individuals were being thrown out of the back exit of the bar. Bottles and glass smashing was heard, along with solid bangs of the furniture. Glancing at the landlord, he was over by the other punters pleading with them not to get involved.

As the easier ones were dealt with, the guys were coming back in to start on the next one. This was a good clear out job. My colleague and I still had a hold on Brian who was shouting at the top of his lungs for his mates.

'Get these ****'s off of me!'

As each of the group were being slung out, I don't think they were in any fit state to even think about coming back in for more. No one else to deal with and my guys were just coming back in and walking towards me.

'Ok Neil, let him go let's have him!' One of them said. I was a bit reluctant. I'd never done this before. Just holding on to someone to wait for a pasting didn't seem right. I would have gladly just slung him out the door telling him he's not welcome back. But this wasn't how it was going to be. I knew it'd be rough, but I didn't think it would be a battering.

'Get off him then' one of them said as they pushed me off him.

This guy just scooped him up off the floor and ploughed his knee into his stomach. Brian's arms went outward to stop some others from moving in, but he was weaker now from being winded. The middle guy grabbed his shirt, pulled his head up and held him up against the wall. With a few choice words, the general gist was that Steve's lads were on the door here now, please leave and never return. I'm guessing you can picture the scenario by now. This wasn't a pleasant experience, but you can't lose face. You have to act up in these situations.

Brian left by the front door because it was closer. As we slung him out I found some bright spark had called the police in. Typical, this would now take some explaining. I was hoping for the removal without their involvement. The landlord knew this, so it must have been a punter who called them. The police were familiar with this sort of situation and remain supportive of any ejections. On this occasion I think they were unaware of what had actually gone on, and merely dealt with the abusive punters who were accusing us of heavy handedness. The guys stayed inside, helping with the arrangement of furniture, while the landlord was pouring the pints out for the lads. It seemed to have gone on without too much hassle. This probably lasted about quarter of an hour in total. One of our guys was then on the phone to Steve saying, 'It's all dealt with, they won't be back here'.

We never had any comeback that night, nor the following night, so the forceful approach seemed to have done the trick. I never thought I'd be part of this kind of world and from this moment saw this line of work in a whole new perspective. A week or so had gone by and things were beginning to settle. The landlord recalled the night frequently saying how well we dealt with it and couldn't thank us enough. He was being a bit annoying, repeating himself all the time, but still at least he was happy.

I was stood at the door one night and my colleague pointed out the girl over the road, calling her the local businesswoman. I didn't get it at first, I'd never been anywhere where prostitution was so obvious, but then I should have guessed by what she was wearing, or should I say lack of it. It was sad to look at her. My colleague on the other hand thought it was highly hilarious that I didn't know what she did and made a bit of a song and dance over it. I didn't want to draw attention to us so moved on inside.

Her name was Lucy. After a few weeks I had made contact with her, offering our services if she ever had a problem with a punter to let us know. My duties at work now included keeping an eye on Lucy over the road. Cars would pull up, chat to her for a bit and she'd get in. She'd give me two kinds of look as the car went by. The first was full of smiles if she was happy, which usually indicated the chap was a regular. The other was an obvious glance of uncertainty. I'd make mental notes of vehicles and descriptions of blokes just in case. I felt a sense of protection for her, not wanting her to be hurt in any way. An hour would go by and she'd be walking up the street, back to her pick up point over the road. Sometimes she'd come to the door to say hello and ask my colleague for a light for her crumpled cigarette.

She never got into any bother while I was there. Just one thing I remember before we move on. She did come to us one time to ask us if we would have a word with a punter as a warning before she went off with him. Looking the man in the eyes I had great delight in telling him that if she didn't come back happy, we had made a note of his vehicle and could easily find out where he lived and he could expect a visit from us to sort him out. I could tell this was a first timer, because he was scared. He lent over towards me offering me the money.

'No you pay her,' I said. With that I walked away from the car back to Lucy and said, 'He's ok. Scared more than anything, but take care and come back here afterwards so I know you're ok'.

'Thanks Neil' she replied and off she went. I often wondered where she'd end up or what state she'd come back in.

Sometimes after a shift, I'd go off for a pint of the black stuff (Guinness) with my colleague. One night we went to our usual after-hours venue, with a different firm on the doors. I got chatting to the doorman there. I found out the name of their firm and posed the question 'What is the boss like?'

Deep down, I had concerns with who I was working for and had questions about some of the methods used. Within a couple of weeks I had changed firms. I was now working with Solent Security and for a guy called Jeff, a six foot five bloke with a northern accent. He seemed friendly enough. He was offering about one pound fifty an hour more than Steve at Pro Security. With an extra twenty or so a week, this was almost an extra eighty pounds a month. This seemed really attractive.

The first location given to me was head doorman for another Irish Bar, just outside of the city centre in a village close to Southampton. This work seemed like fun, with little hassle. No falling around students just a friendly bunch of locals. Usually a Friday and Saturday night, Jeff's guys were asked if they'd finish their pubs at 11.30pm and walk around the corner to the nightclub for a couple of extra hours. Seemed like a good idea to me, so when it was offered I took the extra work happily.

What I was finding after a month or so, was that when something kicked off it was usually big. Very rarely was it just verbal, it must have been something in the beer, cos' this lot used fists to sort out their problems. My training and steady experience with Pro Security was now being put to the test and I found more often than not that I was physically ejecting violent characters without questions. Not always the case, but most of the time, it was already kicking off before I could reason with folks. The confidence and ability in dealing with situations was being demonstrated. A good reputation soon travelled around Solent Security that I was a strong, good and reliable doorman that knew his job. Within a short time, I was moved to the larger venues and extra hours were coming my way. I was probably the richest student in Southampton.

The nightclub I worked at regularly was called 'Marley's'. It was a dark club, with a purple glow about it. The outside of it was a car park. As you walked in the main doors, the person behind the counter who took your entry fee and coats would greet you. Then you'd find yourself walking up the black-carpeted stairs that had LED lights twinkling along the edges. At first this appeared quite nice, but try and imagine the stains on the carpet and dreadfully dated textured wallpaper that had been painted purple. When you got upstairs you saw a quirky building with different levels for different zones. The first seating area to your left was up two steps. Ahead of you was the bar, which ran along the left, after that was the dance floor, which was down two steps. The dance floor was tatty. The DJ booth was over in the right hand corner with the fire exit to the left of him. The dance floor was usually smoke filled and you could have done with the fire brigade issue breathing apparatus to go through it. How all the drunk people got in and out of the dance floor without guide ropes I don't know. We did it because we weren't drunk and knew our bearings. Funny place though. When it kicked off, it kicked off and it was usually full on fighting. The dance floor fire exit was used frequently to eject people. The view was, if they wanted to fight each other they could do it outside. So from the security point of view it was a case of get 'em out and quick.

Jeff, the boss, was head doorman here. Every time I turned up he would always welcome me with a handshake and say 'Usual spot Neil, thanks mate'.

Inside I was just at the top of the stairs watching everyone coming in and keeping an eye on the bar. Jeff was able to poke his head in the door and get the thumbs up signal from me to let him know all was ok inside. For me this was a sign of trust, he knew I had everything on the inside covered. I was in radio link with him and the other security dotted around. The problem with the guy on the dance floor near the DJ was he could never hear us, but we could hear him if he needed us.

One night, all appeared fine until I heard a smash and crash of glasses near the bar area. I walked on over and a woman grabbed me in a panic 'They hit my boyfriend, he's bleeding!' She screamed at me to get the guys that did it. As I walked closer I saw the guy lying on the floor and saw a pool of blood around his head. The floor was a dirty grey vinyl. The blood was dark and spread about the size of his head across the floor. The woman was panicking and hysterical, which I chose to ignore, to just start putting actions in place. I called on the radio to Jeff.

'No one leaves this place, I've got a man injured down by the bar and whoever did it is probably still in here, NO ONE LEAVES! …I need back up at the bar now!'

With that I looked up and a member of bar staff was stood looking over me. I was kneeling by the guy who appeared completely unconscious. I said to the barman, 'Call the police and get an ambulance, don't just stand there'. I leant in close to the guys face, grabbing hold of his hand, I said to him, 'Squeeze my hand bud if can you hear me?' He was out of it, but I could feel the warmth of his breath, 'He's breathing!' I said to the woman.

Looking around again, I saw a security chap. I beckoned him in closer and said to the woman, 'Walk around with him and find the bloke who did it'. I then said to the security bloke, 'The bloke that did this may still be in here, find him! The police are on their way!' The guy on the floor started to come around and I leaned in and said, 'It's ok mate, just lay there, don't get up. Your head is bleeding. Let's get you checked out before you move aye.'

The bloke appeared restless wanting to sit up. Not being able to stop him, he stood up stumbling a bit. He started to walk around holding his head and pushing people out of his way. I managed to grab him and sit him down. The bar man had turned up with a first aid kit. I wasn't concerning myself with a full on bandage, just applying something to try and stop the blood flow. I got out the biggest sterilised dressing I could find and began pressing this on the back of his head. The barman was stood there looking helpless.

'Get out another bandage… and get me some gloves.' I said.

I then said to the bloke, 'Here hold this a minute'. I brought his hand up to his head to hold the bandage himself, and then took the gloves off the barman to put them on. I took over from the bloke and held the bandage on his head allowing him to drop his arm down. The ambulance arrived and the paramedics came in escorted by a security guy. They started attending to him so I headed for the main door to speak to Jeff. 'Did we find him?'

Jeff shrugged his shoulders and said 'No, what's happened in there?' looking me up and down with a concerned look on his face.

'It's ok the blokes fine, but he's had a bottle smashed round his head and the bloke got away with it.' I turned to the woman who was outside shouting at people and said 'If you know who it was, stop causing a scene and report him to the police, they'll be here in a bit'.

Looking back at Jeff, he looked at me and said 'You can't stop these things from happening mate, don't stress about it, it's being sorted now, you did your best'.

My best, the guy got away with it. This was the first time I'd let this stuff get to me, I wanted the guy, but he got away. I was narked off, but not only that, the left sleeve of my jacket was covered from the elbow down in this man's blood. Not just splashes, it was fully coloured in his blood.

'What can we do with this then, are you covering the dry cleaning bill?' I asked Jeff.

He looked at me and said 'Your jacket, your problem'.

Cheek of it, not my fault and a hazard of the job and I had to get it cleaned. I couldn't believe it. This was probably the scariest night I'd had. A real casualty who thankfully lived to tell his story,

but I've got to clean my own jacket, you've gotta be kidding me.
I got home that night and my fiancé looked at me with eyes of fear.
She said, 'What happened?'

Almost like a line from a Bond movie, referring to the blood stained jacket I remember saying the cheesy line of 'Don't worry, it's not mine', as I took the jacket off to show the blood splattered white shirt.

The following day my mates in the house were all interested to hear the story of the night before, looking at the jacket, now dried with a horrendous bloodstain.

A couple of months passed and the manager of Marley's was redecorating into a funky colour filled refit with new rounded furniture and retro décor. About time, I thought, it needed something. Little did I know, he had a different kind of venue in mind.

"I DARE YOU TO DO THAT AGAIN !"

'I DARE YOU TO DO THAT AGAIN !'

05

Matt, the manager of Marleys — fondly known to us as Matt 'The Pratt' had turned his dingy dark purple 'cattle market' into a strip club. How low would this guy go to get a quick buck? The first night the girls were in, the other doorman refused to be anywhere near them, fearing their wives, partners or girlfriends would pop in and see them ogglin' at the girls. Jeff looked at me.

'Neil, do you have a problem with it?'

I admittedly didn't take too long to think about this and agreed to do the close protection for the girls as they danced. Not because I fancied looking, but because I felt a sense of protection for them, taking their personal safety seriously, especially with the sort of blokes who would buy their time.

As the girls would take a guy into the private dance area, my colleagues would spot them walking in and nod at me with their eyebrows raised as if to say, 'Enjoy that one Bird!' Over a period of weeks these girls were beginning to get to know me and appreciate the safety I provided them. They used to comment on the fact that it was never nice to work somewhere where the security were creepy and used to give me hugs and a kiss on the cheek as they left. The other guys would tease me frequently for this, suggesting I was 'in there'. While dancing they used to lean over a guys shoulder pushing their chest into the punters faces and look at me with seductive eyes, slowly drawing me in to their sordid world, but the thing was I was beginning to like it.

Over the weeks we were seeing a different crowd coming in. It mainly consisted of blokes on stag nights, but it also attracted the more affluent customer who'd flash the cash, attracting the girls to them. The girls used to tell me that the money was really the only reason for the work and that they could easily earn a week's wage in a couple of nights dancing. If these girls worked during the day they were doubling their monthly income. One thing I clearly remember was that they never used to turn up in a clapped out motor. It was always the latest sporty hatch or beemer.

One night a punter came up the stairs into the club, with approximately ten people, male and female. This flannel mouthed, smooth talker was obviously minted. Wearing his best bib and tucker, shoes glistening under the lights and commanding the attention of all those around the bar as he began to buy anyone a drink, even the security. I declined, never wanting to drink on duty. I was always aware of professionalism, keeping my head clear and my attention on the job. He seemed to demand a lot of attention from the girls, buying time for his buddies to have a private dance.

Cash was free flowing. Jeff came to the top of the stairs to take a brief glance around. He came to my side, leaned over and asked 'Everything going ok in here?' All was fine that night except my inquisitive mind as to who this guy was.

'Who's that then? Do you know who he is?'

Jeff said, 'Don't you? That's a Saints footballer'

I forget the bloke's name. I was never into football, even now, it's never been of any interest to me. Now it all made sense, the amount of flowing cash and the mates, all using him for drinks and a bit of the high life.

Towards the end of the night, I saw him talking to one of the girls, who was glancing over at me constantly. I began to frown as if to ask what's up? She walked away from him and he looked over towards his group of friends. She walked over to another girl and started talking to her, with hand gestures and pointing over at the guy with his group. I was looking back at him, wondering what was going on? She walked back over to him and said something. He looked over at me, I could see his lips moving, but the music was so loud I couldn't hear a thing. I guessed it was a 'is that him' type response because he began to wander over to me. Not knowing what to expect, what followed came as a bit of a surprise. He walked up to me, introduced himself and spoke to me with the utmost respect. He began to enlighten me as to what this last few minutes had all been about. It was about two in the morning and the club was about to finish but he wanted to party on into the night with his friends.

He went on to ask, 'I'm wondering if you'd do me a huge favour?'

I was thinking I hardly knew the bloke and he's asking me for favours? Where was this going I wondered?

'I've asked one of the girls whether they want to earn a bit more cash and continue dancing for us. We're going off to a curry house for some grub and I'm asking them if they'll come along and provide the entertainment. The thing is, they won't do it unless you're there. So can you help us out here mate and come along as well? I'll buy you a curry, sort out the transport to get you and the girls home and pay for your time, what do you say?'

Well if the girls wanted me there I thought they must be happy to do it. Even though they hadn't been any trouble at all during the evening, my thinking was, not on my own I'm not.

'Two secs, let me speak to my boss' I said tapping him on his arm. I walked downstairs to speak to Jeff. Outside I asked Jeff what I should do.

He replied with a care free attitude 'Neil it's not up to me, you wanna do it, go ahead, it's up to you. He's alright he'll cough up too.'

I was now thinking who to ask, Dave seemed like the obvious choice, so I walked passed the footballer and onto the dance floor towards the DJ booth to speak to him. 'Hey Dave, you up for some work after hours? There's a curry in it?' I asked.

He looked slightly puzzled, but shrugged his shoulders and agreed, 'Ah whatever, always up for a curry!'

I then explained to him what we were doing and said 'How much should we get out of this guy for this?'

Dave began to smile and said 'A ton each'.

I thought this would be a bit steep but then thought the amount he'd been splashing around that evening it was probably not that much to him, but a ton in my pocket would be a nice little bonus.

Walking back to our footballer, I said to him, 'I ain't going on my own with you lot, I've no idea what you're going to get up to, it's gotta be two of us at a ton each'.

Thinking he'd put up a bit of resistance to the price he surprised me when he said 'Brilliant mate, spot on. I'll see you're alright and you can drink and eat whatever you want it's on me alright!'

With that I turned to Dave and put my thumb up to indicate it was all agreed. Another fifteen minutes and we were going for an extra earner. The girls were smiling too. My guess was they'd bartered for an extra earner for the work too. This was a bonus for all of us, and we got two beautiful girls to look after.

Fifteen minutes later and we were walking down the stairs with the girls and being led out by the footballer and his following flock.

As we walked outside, we were greeted by two limos, one for the footballer and us and the other for his lower mates. He wanted a private limo dance with his hired girls. Dave and I let the girls carry on with their job and we sat there thinking what a strange night this was going to be. We turned up to a curry house and the Asian guys in the restaurant came to the door and unlocked them. They'd already closed up. While the footballer was paying to keep them open for another hour or so, I was putting my jacket around one of the girls who was looking rather cold in her lack of warm clothes. We went in and the footballer was calling the shots and telling his mates who was getting the first dance. He turned to his left and called over to the staff, 'Get these two guys a beer' (referring to Dave and I). They came over like servants. We looked and behaved like the hired heavies and the restaurant staff genuinely looked slightly scared by the experience, running around to get our food orders and drinks as quick as possible. The dancers were doing their thing between courses and Dave and I were enjoying the night too. This was an easy earner.

When the girls had had enough and done their thing for each of them, that was it, they wanted out. The footballer walked over to Dave and I and leant in between us. He started counting out the twenty pound notes.

'One hundred… two hundred and here's a third for being spot on guys thanks for your help lads. I really do mean it, thanks for your time guys… and here's an extra £30 for your taxi to get the girls back.'

We'd earned £150 each, had a few pints and a curry just for sitting there and doing very little, just so he could keep his little party going for a few more hours. If only all jobs paid out this well.

A couple of months went by and all was rolling on well. The girls were known on first name terms and the banter flowed between us well. We had a good working relationship, even to the point where I was paying them for my own private dances at the end of the shift. One day I was walking through the city's main shopping centre with my fiancé when one of the girls walked past me and said cheerfully,

'Hiya Neil.'

Tina turned to me with a certain kind of look. Guys know this look well. It's a 'she's prettier than me look' and a 'do you fancy her?' type analysis that blokes often fall into the trap of. Stumbling into it and then making a pigs ear of it, often resulting in a brief domestic and ending after the next few hours of the silent treatment. Fortunately, I think I batted this one off ok. I replied casually by lying.

'Oh, she's one of the bar staff at the club'.

The fact I had seen her completely nude and even had her dance for me, made me somewhat extremely uncomfortable. I could feel this butterfly feeling and sickness, my throat felt tight.

It was that guilty feeling I never wanted to ever feel again. After this day my private dances stopped and I came clean with her about where I worked. Until now she never had a clue, but I explained to her that the guilt of not telling her was doing me in and that I felt like I was leading a secret life. I never thought she'd respond with such an acceptance, but she did. In fact she seemed to enjoy the fact that I worked there? This puzzled me somewhat, but it made it almost acceptable. So the work there continued.

The manager, Matt, had managed to get the venue lined up for the Daily Sport Tour. How he did this I'll never know, but a month later we were going to have the girls from the well known newspaper visiting the venue and we were to be the security for the job. The word got about and we heard the club was listed in the paper for all their readers to see.

The night arrived and there were no girls in sight. The promoter or 'Sport Tour Co-ordinator' was talking to Matt at the end of the bar and glancing over at us guys. We were stood in our usual places waiting for the punters to come in. Jeff was holding them at the door. There was a queue of about twenty guys. Some of them had a Sport newspaper under their arms for the cheap entry price of a tenner. Those who didn't know about the 'bring-a-paper' discount had to pay double to get in.

The doors opened and the guys began coming up the stairs. It must have been a bit of an anti-climax with all the build up outside.

The anticipation of seeing a bevy of beauties as they entered the club led to an anti-climax, because none of the girls were there. The only people they got to see were the usual female bar staff that all looked like they were sucking on lemons, not really wanting to be at work that night at all. The other people they got to see, were us, a bunch of heavies eyeballing each of them to try and suss out who were potential aggro. Some of these guys looked uncomfortable, sat there drinking a pint of lager. The average age was late twenties to early thirties. The sort that had more money than sense and more often than not, were not married or hooked up with a girl of their own. If they had, they probably wouldn't even be there in the first place.

It was 9.30pm, the punters had waited over an hour and were told by the DJ to sit back and enjoy the music as the girls were going to arrive in a short while. A VIP styled van pulled up outside and the girls rolled out to meet the tour co-ordinator at the bottom of the stairs. Jeff called Dave and I downstairs to escort the girls to the dance floor area, and the mayhem began. Dave set off back towards the bar and I stood in the middle of the dance floor with a circle of chairs around me. The girls wandered into the crowd and picked their victims, pulling them up to the dance floor and sitting them on the seats. The DJ started a music track and the fifteen quid dance by one of these girls lasted the length of that song. Tops four minutes, but on average just three minutes. This went on for about an hour and a half. Then a couple of the girls did a dance to the general crowd in the club, but that was about it. Money was flowing and these girls were raking it in. No trouble during the night, a few excitable lads, but nothing major.

I went home that night and told the lads who lived in my house what had gone on that night, I remember sitting down at the dining table with a piece of paper working out how many times the girls stripped down to their birthday suits, the number of girls, and the frequency of the songs for the one and a half hours. I don't want to revisit the maths, but it was a crazy amount and at the time a talking point with the other doorman too.

The following night we turned up for a more normal night of the usual. Jeff was stood at the door greeting us as we arrived. But he held us at the door till we were all there so he could have a word with us.

'Last night lads, was spot on. We pulled it off lads and the tour manager liked the way we did things. He's asked us to do the same again in Brighton tomorrow night. They are in Portsmouth tonight, but already have a firm for that one, but he was impressed with us and wants us to do Brighton, so are we all up for it? I'm up'ing the rate for this one cos it's a bit of a drive, and I'll sort cover for this place, what do you say lads?'

Most of us smiled and said yeah, but one wouldn't. He 'didn't fancy the drive' was the reason, but the guys all chipped in and suggested he had trouble with the missus for last night and he didn't want to push it for another night. As we went on in there were no punters at all. The resident girls were moaning because their usual crowd had spent their weekly budget on last night's entertainment. It was a quiet night and the girls were sat on bar stools moaning to anyone who'd listen. Matt did the honourable thing and coughed up a bit of cash to pay them for their wasted time.

The next evening we were off to Brighton. We received a quick tour of the building by Jeff who was already there as we arrived. He was going around giving us a tour of all the fire exits, extinguishers, cameras, first aid kits and so on. We were given our positions for the evening and I had the usual close protection duty of staying with the girls. The night was almost a replica of the night back at our club. The girls turned up later than expected and did their thing as before.

There was only one problem, a guy in his late twenties, with fair hair and wandering hands. It was a given rule that when a girl danced for a bloke, the bloke was to keep his hands by his sides and not to touch them. This one chap placed his hands on the girl's thigh and began raising his hand higher towards her butt cheek. She grabbed his hand firmly and placed it back by his side. I took one step and she put her hand up to me to stop me from moving in. I eyeballed the bloke, pointing at my eyes and then pointing at him. I then waved my hands at him to gesture to him keep the hands off. He waved quickly, apologising. Within thirty seconds, he did it again and the girl backed off him and stood back. I moved in and stood nice and close to him, leaning in I said firmly, 'I dare you to do that again, I'm telling you now, keep your hands to yourself.'

He apologised again. The girl thanked me and proceeded to continue her dance for him. Within another thirty seconds or so the hand had grabbed her thigh for the last time.

The girl backed off him, I could hear her muttering saying things like 'That's not on, he shouldn't be touching me', as she looked at the girls dancing for other punters next to her.

As soon as she'd backed off I had moved in and I was ready for this. I'd been watching him like a hawk. Behind his head was a chrome railing that circled the dance floor. To grab him and walk him to the exit seemed like a long way around. My size gave me the advantage on this one as I grabbed his belt buckle and the scruff of his shirt around his chest. I lifted him out of his seat and threw him over the railing. Landing in a heap on the floor it took him a second to get to his knees. Looking up at me he began shouting.

'What was that for, there was no need for that!'

He went on ranting. Dave and Jeff moved in and Jeff said with a smile to me, 'This guy leaving then Neil is he?'

'He's outta here, he can't keep his hands off the girl and I warned him he'd be going.'

He was in the building for all of thirty minutes or so. It cost him a tenner to get in and fifteen quid for the dance, no doubt the beer wasn't cheap either, and he didn't even get to the end of his dance and he was leaving. Jeff had no patience for idiots and manhandled the guy toward the exit. This club was also upstairs, like our regular venue, and as they approached the stairs Dave and Jeff lifted him off his feet projecting him down the stairs. A sense of guilt ran through me. I'd already manhandled him, so I didn't see the point of throwing him down a set of stairs too. Jeff and Dave looked over at me and stuck their thumbs up in a 'sorted' kinda way. At this point I was slightly distracted by the potential casualty at the bottom of the stairs instead of keeping an eye on the girls. Mind you, I don't think anyone was going to be daft enough to even touch the girls from here on. The rest of the night went off without a hitch. Funny that.

The relationship with Jeff continued to improve. Jeff began to speak to me about confidential matters that other guys were left out of the loop of, as it didn't concern them at this point. The trust level from him of me was increasing, to the point where he saw me as a good guy to have around. The same thing happened with the previous firm where I was beginning to get moved around for clean up jobs. All I would have liked is to stay in one place, possibly as head doorman, running my own place with my own team of guys. I guessed it may happen one day.

Anyway the clean up job was here. It turned out to be a Chinese restaurant. 'A restaurant?' I thought, strange venue for a clean up.

'What needs cleaning up Jeff, dishes? Why us, what's the problem there?'

Jeff went on to expand on the job spec and in his joking response said 'Shut up! It's a Chinese restaurant downstairs but upstairs it's a club. It's the club that has the problems, but the manager has been told he'll be shut down if they can't stop the drug problem going on.'

This was a stop and search job. Should be fun I thought. Jeff continued 'It's not the users he wants, there are dealers in there and he wants them prosecuted. So we have to hold on to them and call for the police lads, got it?' No problem, this was going to be a fun one.

After a couple of nights of doing searches, I suspected one guy and told him to stand against the wall so I could search him. As I finished the previous guy off, I was watching this suspect guy look a tad agitated. Rummaging in his pockets I could sense something was up. I stood in front of him and this guy couldn't give me one glance of eye contact. I spoke to him like I had done the others, asking him various questions for my own safety, like the potential of sharps on his person that may harm me and the like. He grunted in response. I reached into his sweater pocket and pulled out a bag of pills, he moved his arm quickly knocking them out of my hand. They dropped to the floor, he bent down quickly and grabbed the gear and bolted for the door. I tried to grab him but he was moving very quickly. I gave chase and ran out of the building after him. Some people may not know this about me, but I can run very fast, surprising anyone who gets to see this phenomenon. Dave was with me on the door and came running too. At last a colleague followed me when he needed to … and I didn't even need to ask this time! As I turned to the right of the building a taxi driver was parked in the road and had just dropped off a couple, who were paying for their journey at the driver's door window. The dealer ran into the parked taxi and was heard shouting at the driver.

'Drive!'

But the reaction from the driver was not as responsive as he'd hoped. As I approached the vehicle I grabbed the offside rear door opening it, the dealer got out the nearside and started running again. I shouted at the taxi driver not to drive off as he may have planted stuff in the car and we would need to search it. Dave was now giving chase on the dealer down the street and I went running after them. Dave eventually tripped the guy up and jumped on him. In a scuffle of arms and legs flapping around everywhere, I joined in and we grabbed the guy in a wristlock, brought him to his feet, bringing him back towards the restaurant. The taxi driver waited, and said to me   'What's going on, why have you told me the police want to search my vehicle, I don't know this man.'

Pointing at the dealer who was doubled over with his arms raised up behind his back, I said to the taxi guy that I realised he was innocent, but the guy who I was holding had drugs on his person and may have hid some in his car.

By this time the Police had been called and responded with immediate effect. They turned up, cuffed the guy and had now taken over the situation. Two officers began stripping the taxi down, boot open, seats moved about and a full on search was taking place. The taxi driver was beginning to give off a bit of aggro to the officers as the time taken to do this was stopping him from earning a living. I almost felt sorry for the guy, but couldn't help to chuckle with Dave about it. The dealer was put in the back of a police car and the officers took statements from us both. We'd got the regular guy and the management were more than happy with us, giving us free grub at the end of the night, eating with the other staff.

After a good night, the next day I heard some bad news. Jeff the boss was arrested for GBH and intimidating a witness. He'd only taken a witness down a dark alley and given 'em a frightener to not dump him in it in court, fearing he'd go down for a previous charge of assault. Daft bloke just sealed his 'go to jail card', no collecting two hundred notes for passing 'Go', just go directly to jail and no get out of jail card was going to help him this time. He was going in for some time.

Business went into the hands of his heavies, who in fairness had no clue how to do proper business other than be mindless thugs. They had no respect for the staff they had and were beginning to lose guys fast. I was looking elsewhere too. I wanted out, their attitude stank. Weekly payment was also coming up wrong and frequently needed sorting, but the guys were real nuisances and often said 'Tough, like it or lump it'. So one day, far over due, I was off.

"NEVER
BEEN
PUNCHED"

'NEVER BEEN PUNCHED' 06

It was now 1999 and I was in the final year of my studies. They were not affected too much as I used to do assignments during the day at the University library in between lectures. I was never a true academic and you would often see me in the library looking up books like 'Economics for Dummies' or 'How to bluff your way through Law'.

The thing with doing this sort of work was it got in your head and it was hard to switch off. If you're a doorman or security guard reading this, how many times have you walked into a bar or nightclub and looked around you thinking... Where are the fire extinguishers and fire exits? Where are the security cameras? Where are the security guards? Do you assess other punters behaviour? If you ever go in a club do you take a few minutes to look around the room and work out which doorman is talking to who on the radio? How many there are? And are you on the look out for potential trouble, thinking you'll lend 'em a hand if they can't handle it?

I'm writing this book around ten years later and I still do it. I find it hilarious walking in a venue and seeing the young security fellas acting up, making out they are hard as nails. Recently one chap decided to make himself comfortable by jumping up onto a stack of chrome patio chairs, when he got to the top, the chairs buckled under the strain and leaned over tipping him off. As I walked out of the venue, seeing this I smirked at the guy thinking 'you plank!' Trying to look casual and then he goes and does that.

My fiancé and I were in a famous department store doing all the usual gift shopping a couple of weeks before Christmas. I'm a typical bloke when it comes to shopping. If it can be done in one shop all the better, in and out with the minimum of fuss. On this occasion, I was stood in the queue to pay. There were two lines of people and Tina and I were stood in one of the lines with our arms full of stuff. I spotted in the other line, two young looking lads with a party box of eight bottled alcopops. You know the sort, Hooch, WKD, Breezers. As I was stood there I said to Tina, 'If that lad gets served I'll ask her why she didn't ask for I.D. He's clearly underage.' She was oblivious as to what was going on and answered her phone whilst balancing the stuff in her other arm.

I was about four customers away from the till, watching these lads like a hawk, not taking my eye off them. They got to the counter and she rightly challenged them for I.D. She checked with her manager and the manager agreed they looked too young. As she began to take the bottles away from them, the lad was overheard saying.

'I can see you're really busy, do you want me to put that back for you?'

She smiled at him and said, 'Oh if you wouldn't mind that'll be great, thanks.'

I was stood there thinking, what has she just done, he's now just going to walk out with it anyway. Sure enough the lad was heading for the exit. I dumped the armful of stuff on Tina and said 'Hold on to this a sec.'

What was initially an armful for her was now a pile that covered her face, as she couldn't see over the height of the load. I began to follow these guys. Now then, you may realise that for it to be theft they need to have left the building with the goods without paying. So, I knew that I couldn't do anything until they had left the main doors. As I was picking up pace to catch up with them, I wanted to be as discrete as possible. I took a step sideways to scooch past an elderly lady who looked shocked by the fact I'd got so close, making an 'Ooo' sound as I passed. Realising I'd made her jump I apologised. Looking at her, I then proceeded to put my back end into a seven-foot high display of neatly stacked Barbie dolls, which toppled over crashing to the floor in front of the woman. I looked at her realising what I had done. I looked back at the lads who were alerted by the fallen Barbies. They saw me and placed the bottles on the floor. Looking at me they then took two or three steps and walked out of the store leaving the bottles on the floor. As they walked out laughing, I knew that was it, I'd blown it. I looked back at the old lady and the look on her face was of sheer shock. By now this cock-up had attracted quite an audience. I look back on this moment fondly as one of my most embarrassing moments. Barbies of all things, it could have been anything else but Barbies, why Barbies!

Let's get this back on track. After Solent Security's employee neglect from the numpties Jeff had left in charge, I'd phoned Steve at Pro Security to see if he had anything available. He had a head doorman position for me at a newly acquired venue. He promised me that he wouldn't move me about and that this venue would be mine for as long as I wanted it.

Steve's new venue was Yates, the pub and restaurant chain, working for a manager called Keith. He was a short bloke, but a ruthless shrewd businessman. He'd either been managing pubs for years and was the start-up manager for new sites, or he had a background in business and wanted to take this on as a challenge. As for us, we were in for the opening night and had a group talk with Keith and the rest of the bar staff before the doors opened for the first time.

He had a clear idea of how he wanted his pub run. Our objective was 100% no agro.

'Any hassle, get em' out, I don't want 'em in here!'

Let me take a short moment to introduce the team. Firstly and probably most importantly there was Frank. Frank was a diamond geezer. He was trained in tai-kwon-do and was not shy in the quiet moments of the night, to show off his roundhouse kicks that would clearly knock any six foot tall bloke to the floor. He would often demonstrate his wrist holds and arm locks on me. He was good and knew his job. He had a secret smile very few people saw. Inside was car sales Paul, traffic warden by day Pete, then Mike and bald Jon. I had the utmost respect for these guys. They were all mature guys, professional at their jobs and enjoyed their work.

Frank and I would stand at the main door greeting the punters and stopping the undesirables. If you have ever been stopped for coming into a venue because of dress code, it's usually because the doorman doesn't like the look of you. Rather than making this known to you they use any excuse to find a reason to stop you from entering the premises. We'd often be saying quietly to the other, 'trainers', 'no ripped jeans' 'no football shirts' just to find that alternative reason not to let someone in.

I used to think of us two as being the good and bad cop pair. I was the polite one who'd think about customer service and professionalism. Frank was the agro sorter. I had the follow technique sorted and this venue was well suited to this. Frank and I had a tight control on the problem cases. The security guys inside were the eyes. When they saw something they'd tell me. Frank and I wanted to know everything that went on. They reported in via radio and I would go in and approach the problem customer asking them to pop to the front door where we could talk as the music was too loud inside, which amazed Frank every time. Not having to manhandle someone to leave was a new concept to him. Of course this wasn't always going to work. One day I walked to the main doors, turned around and the chap never followed me.

Frank said 'Is it my turn?'

I laughed and waved my hands as a gesture for him to go on in.

I radioed Pete, 'Neil to Pete, Neil to Pete.' I waited for the acknowledgment.

'Go Ahead.'

'Yeah Pete, Frank's on his way in, point out the chap to him please and give him a hand bringing him to the door, cheers mate'.

'Will do' came his reply.

Probably thirty seconds went by and I saw through the glazed doors Frank and a bit of a scuffle heading towards me. I opened the door and the guy flew past me stumbling and landing on the floor.

'When my pal here wants you to come to the door, you do the right thing and come to the door!' said Frank, 'Was this the guy?' he asked as he looked at me pointing his thumb at him.

'Yeah, there's no point talking to him.' I changed my focus from Frank to the punter on the floor 'You had the nice option but you chose to ignore it, so cheerio pal.' The man got up off the floor and tried to start a conversation, asking why he'd been chucked out. 'Let's get this straight, I came in there to speak to you but you chose to ignore me, so now you get the same treatment from me, now clear off.' He went off ranting down the street shouting to any member of the public he could, accusing us of being heavy handed. This was the way Frank and I worked. It worked well.

Another night and another punter was asked to come outside for a chat. This one followed me and asked, 'What's up mate?'

First off, I hate being called mate by people I have never met before. If you the reader do this, think about how it sounds and that if you say it to the wrong person it will not work in your favour. Anyhow, I told this guy he was being politely asked to move on and that he was not re-entering the building. He began to act up and started pushing past me to get in. Frank blocked him and pushed him back into the street. I walked the guy to the far edge of the building.

'You're trying my patience and my colleague doesn't do nice.'

He started to talk over me, so I shouted louder to get his attention,

'Listen to me, I'm doing you a favour by talking. All I have to do is let him off his leash and he'll end this right now. How do you want it, walk away with a bruised ego? Or a kick off in the street?'

'Come on then' he said.

I looked over my shoulder towards Frank, who at this point knew it wasn't working out. He started to take his jacket off. He screwed it up into a ball and then threw it on the floor. I wouldn't treat my jacket like this, but this was Frank. He then started to roll up his sleeves and began beckoning for the guy to come over to him. What made me chuckle was the guy came off his high horse from the potential reality of being battered and shook my hand, apologised and fled pretty sharp. I laughed, as did Frank, as he picked up his jacket from the floor.

'What a prat, he was really winding me up,' said Frank.

The nights in Southampton were cold. On this job I used to wear a long black woollen coat for some warmth. The leather gloves were also a necessity. These were provided by one of our chaps, Pete, who usually stood on the stairs. He claimed to the 'police issue desk' that he kept on losing pairs of gloves, just to get another pair for Frank and I. We were fully appreciative of these gloves, especially in the hard winter nights. The bitter wind used to whistle down through the main High Street and cut us in half.

Banning people was always a pleasure. When you ban someone you know the next few weeks you'll have a bit of fun keeping the persistent banee from entering the premises when your back is turned, or dealing with their mates on the inside who were letting them in a fire exit. When doing a walkabout inside, part of the head doorman's job was to see who was in the building and watch attitudes and behaviour. We'd banned a young lad who would constantly wind up the doorman inside. He was chucked out twice for the same reason in a matter of days, so Frank had little patience with the guy and told him he was banned and to clear off. It was Christmas time and this was his regular, so he constantly hassled the management and us about being let back in. We wouldn't let up. We'd had enough of his stupid behaviour.

It was New Years Eve and the doors were locked until 7pm. The punters had formed a typically British queue outside, of easily a hundred or so. We arrived at 6.30pm and had a staff meeting. This was a ticket only venue where the punters had all paid ten quid to enjoy an evening with a guest DJ and live music by a popular tribute band. It was going to be a good night. After this short meeting we were wiring ourselves up with the mics and radios. I turned to Frank and said, 'Guess who's in the queue'.

Frank didn't do guessing games.

'Who, Craig David?' he sarcastically replied.

I laughed and said, 'It's only that pillock who keeps trying to get in.'

'You're kidding, it's a ticket entry and he's got a ticket, what a prat'. Frank replied.

I turned to the manager Keith and asked, 'How long have they been queuing?'

'They've been there for about an hour.'

Both Frank and I laughed out loud, and looked at each other. I said, 'Are we going to tell him not to bother queuing?'

Frank smirked and said 'No, let him queue and we'll turn him away at the door. Let him waste his time, let him think he's got a chance, we'll let him take one step in and then pull him out'.

As we opened the doors at 7pm, we started ripping tickets in half and telling punters that the first drink was free. They needed to hand in half of the ticket to the bar to get their drinks. As we collected tickets and checked a few ID's we let people in slowly, holding the line up while we put tickets in pockets and checked the ages. Our banned friend was about halfway down the queue and it was about 7.15pm when he eventually got to the door. He had queued up for well over forty-five minutes, possibly up to an hour. He was wearing a white t-shirt and a pink cowboy hat with a glittery star on it. Frank took the tickets and I was checking ID's of all the people who walked in. As Frank ripped his ticket in half the guy thought he was in and then he got to me. At this point he put his head down and swiftly went for the door. I stopped him, pulled off his hat and grabbed his arm.

'You are doing my swede in, how many times have we got to tell you, you're barred, go party somewhere else.'

It was almost cruel, his mates had all got in and you could see the disappointment in his eyes. He argued for a short while complaining he'd bought a ticket and wanted a refund. Frank wasn't too polite with this one and told him where he could go. His mates were stood at the door beckoning him to try and get in, but he shrugged his shoulders.

'They won't let me.'

He began to call us a familiar name that we got called whenever we upset folks, which is unprintable. But we continued to smile, which tended to wind them up further.

'In or out? You're blocking the door, move, which way?' I said to his mates.

They went in under protest and the guy walked off, his head low. Frank and I laughed, but deep down I almost felt sorry for the lad. It was the biggest night of the year and he was going to be partying alone without his mates. The night itself went off without a hitch and was probably the best night we'd ever had. I think the ticket purchase idea worked. Only those who wanted to be there were. It stopped the riff raff from going in.

We never had any major brawls there. It was merely stupid behaviour, which resulted in people getting ejected. The way Frank and I had control of the ejections meant that the security inside had an easy job. They only needed to get involved when we wanted them. Admittedly, sometimes they had to act first and eject someone. On these occasions, we got a radio call from one of our boys saying that someone was on their way. Frank and I would open the doors and see a body flying through the air and hitting the floor with a thud. We'd close the doors and stand side by side, blocking any way of getting back in.

One night, all appeared normal but this one I remember clearly. It was a packed out Saturday night and I walked in to do a usual walk around. As I returned towards the door I saw a guy standing very close to the wall looking into a corner. I couldn't believe my eyes. This guy was urinating up the wall. Without hesitation, I grabbed the guy around the neck and began to drag him towards the door. I struggled with the guy. When Frank realised he opened the door and lent a hand. When we got him outside he tucked his manhood away and began pointing, shouting at me very aggressively. As Frank was holding the guy back, he turned to me and asked, 'What's this one unhappy about?'

'The filthy git was having a slash in the corner of the bar, there's no need for it.' I said with a feeling of anger brewing.

The guy was not letting up, and was beginning to get more aggressive, pushing and shoving Frank. Frank didn't take much of this kind of behaviour, so grabbed his shirt and pulled him into the doorway where no CCTV could film what was about to take place. Now in the doorway this guy was about to get it, Frank laid into him with arms flying everywhere. Frank swept at the guy's legs, taking him down to the floor and grabbed his face. The guy had fear in his eyes as Frank's fingers were strongly, and no doubt painfully, being pressed into his face. I stood out of the doorway in the street keeping a lookout. As a police car approached I told Frank I was calling them over so they could deal with him. As the WPC approached I tapped Frank's shoulder.

'Ease off now.' I said to him.

He grabbed the guy's arm and pulled him from the doorway, dragging him into the street. A bit of a scuffle occurred as we locked him up ready to be handcuffed by the police officers. Keith was waiting by the door puzzled at what had gone on. The WPC looked up at Frank and I and said, 'What's he done?'

I told her, and Keith chipped in saying 'I'm sending him a cleaning bill.'

She then placed the guy under arrest for being drunk and disorderly in a public place. He got taken off in the van and he was out of the way. Keith was not a happy chap, shouting at us for allowing it to happen in the first place. When he'd gone in out of the way, Frank assured me it was not our fault and we acted as quick as we could.

There is something strange about the world of the doorman. It is all about connections and respect. It's a handshake culture. Those who respected us, gave us a handshake, those who we respected we gave them a handshake. Watch any of the major gangster movies and it'll have numerous handshake scenes. It always reminds me of my time in Southampton. To us, the ones who we respected didn't need to queue. They could bypass the queue leaving the rest of the crowd to wait. They got the VIP treatment. They'd expect it and we gave it to them.

Let me introduce one chap we called Spike. His name was Stu or Big Stu, but I nicknamed him Spike, after his dental surgery. He also looked a bit like the bulldog cartoon character from the cartoon Tom and Jerry. He was big, well over 6ft, and only needed his big hands to squeeze a guy by the throat to get their attention. He always used to ask if we were ok as he shook our hands at the door.

He always used to say, 'Anything I can do for you lads I'm here to help out if you need me'. It was always nice to know you had heavy backup if all went a bit 'Pete Tong'.

Patting me on the shoulder as he walked in one night, Frank leant in and called him back to the door. He asked him something quietly in his ear. They talked to each other looking into the bar area. Frank came back out to the door.

'You know that guy who had some attitude earlier, Stu's going to sort it.' I remember thinking, what's going to happen next?

Within seconds of being told by Frank, the doors slammed open, which made me jump. I stood to one side, as did Frank. Stu had grabbed the guy by the back of the neck and with his vice like grip was lifting him almost off his feet. Holding his other arm, Stu was walking the guy across the road and proceeded to walk into the dark park opposite.

I turned to Frank and said, 'What's he gonna do with him?'.

'I asked him to sort him out, I've had enough of his attitude', he said. Frank and I couldn't take our eyes of the dark trees of the public park opposite, waiting for Stu to come back out.

About a minute later, Stu came out, glanced left and right as he dodged traffic and walked towards us. He said one word and tapped Frank on his arm as he walked back in to his awaiting pint.

'Sorted'.

I looked at Frank and said, 'What's he done to him?'

'Don't ask' was his reply.

I looked over the road in the hope of seeing the guy surface and waddle off home, but he never came out of the park, at least not from the pub side. There were many exits he could have taken, I just hoped the police wouldn't turn up with questions about a guy who had been violently attacked and left unconscious or even worse found dead in the park. Nothing ever did come back from this, but for a short while I worried a lot about the guy. He didn't deserve a pasting from Big Stu.

It was now coming to the end of my time in Southampton, and my time doing door work was also coming to a close. Frank and the guys arranged a night out to send me off. We had a good laugh, drinking heavily and getting taxi's home. I got so plastered I barely remembered it. But my housemates remembered it well. The drunken results were captured on a camcorder that was shown to me the following day. This provided plenty of amusement for the guys I lived with for many days.

In the last week of the studies I remember the tutor asking all the students about plans for the Graduation Ceremony. When he came to me, I remember calling from the back of the lecture theatre.

'I won't be there, could you stick the certificate in the post.'

The look from my fellow students was of shock.

'Why?' some called out.

I couldn't be bothered with any ceremonial presentation of the certificate. It wasn't high on my list of importance and I didn't see what all the fuss would be about. As for wearing those stupid robes and a bit of cardboard on your head, no, I was not doing it.

In the three years of doing this job, it was a proud fact that I'd managed to come out unscathed. Ok, on occasions I may have acted first and asked questions later, but to be ahead of the rest was always important. The aim was not to get hurt and to stop others from getting hurt too. I always managed to talk people out of a problem or when needed, used my training to protect others and myself from any harm. For me, it wasn't about violence and aggro, but more about doing a job professionally and with the minimal of aggro and incidents, keeping punters safe on their nights out. Whilst in Southampton I had grown in confidence and skills when dealing with conflict. Three years on the doors and I had never been punched. I'm guessing not many doormen could say this.

Leaving Southampton, Tina and I got married on the 6th July 2000 in Somerset, about a month after the graduation. It was the culmination of a year's worth of planning. We then moved to Essex later in the summer of 2000. This was the beginning of a new life for Neil Bird. However, it was short lived with a shocking end just three years later.

'WHAT DO THESE MUPPETS WANT?'

'WHAT DO THESE MUPPETS WANT?'

We were driving home from work one day and I looked at Tina's hand on the steering wheel. I noticed she wasn't wearing her wedding or her engagement ring. This was out of the ordinary because she never took them off, not even to do any cleaning. When I asked why she wasn't wearing them, she replied, 'They are probably in the bathroom', and explained that she had probably taken them off that morning and forgotten to put them back on. I thought it was odd that she had taken them off, but didn't have any concerns that it was for any other reason.

Some days later after a day at work, I walked in swinging my bag towards the dining table. I saw Tina sitting at the bottom of the stairs and said, 'Hiya you ok?' What she said next floored me.

'I want a divorce.'

You know, the reason why this comes up in the book as a bolt out of the blue, is because that is exactly what happened. I had moved to a village in Essex after purchasing our first home, for Tina to further her career in teaching. There is nothing to write about regarding the relationship, because it was normal. As far as

I thought, we were ok. We had banter and fun together. We had some differences in opinion as would any couple, but we hardly ever argued. Arguing was something I refused to do. I think in the seven years we were together we had about five or six arguments, if that. But these didn't lead up to this. I had no explanation for her determined decision to end it.

I grew up with Christian values about marriage and having seen my own parents go through a divorce, I knew this was not what I wanted. I could understand differences needing to be worked out, but this seemed definite. I told her that divorce was not even an option and that counselling would need to be sought first. I asked her what had brought her to this decision, but I never got a valid reason for this drastic action. So, I refused to accept that this was what was going to happen. I was determined to not let it happen. I told her that I would get out of her hair for a week or so for her to have time to think about what she was asking. I went to Somerset on my own and visited the family. It was close to my Dad's birthday, which gave an explanation for the visit. We had kept in touch by phone and a week later, a day after my birthday, Tina had given the go ahead to come home and try and sort things out.

As a bloke, when something like this comes up, you can't help but think it's got something to do with you. Are you treating her right, buying flowers, doing your fair share around the house, putting the rubbish out, showing appreciation and giving enough hugs. When I returned to Essex, I made a point of doing extra stuff around the house, like cleaning, vacuuming etc. Even preparing good home-cooked meals, buying in fresh food and buying in special ingredients for that special touch. I can cook, I enjoy cooking, I realised I never did much of it, so I thought it was partly this lack of involvement around the home that had caused the relationship to collapse. During the month of May I did everything I could to try and restore the broken relationship.

Mid June, it came up again. All I did to try and bring the love and support back in to our relationship hadn't worked. She came to me with that look again. I had that gut wrenching feeling that I knew what was coming.

'It's no good, I haven't changed my mind. I thought I could. It's not you it's me.' It's what everyone hears, when ultimately you feel it has everything to do with you, regardless of what they say.

'I want a divorce, I'm sorry.'

Her outlook on life had changed and I didn't feature in any part of it. At this point I tried to argue the point that I wasn't prepared to have a failed marriage. I pulled out the yellow pages and started looking for marriage guidance counsellor phone numbers. She told me point blank that there was no point and that it wouldn't change her mind. In sheer frustration the voices began rising. I was being stubborn for as long as I could. This lasted for hours. But it came to the point where I'd had enough and I couldn't stick it any longer. I was going. I was beginning to pack a bag. I was off to Somerset again. This time she had as long as it took me to file a divorce to stop it from going through. I had it in my head, that if she wanted one I'd be the one filing for it based on unreasonable behaviour. As I began packing the car, I remember seeing my neighbour pull up in his car. He saw me, asked if everything was ok and I told him what was happening. He looked shocked and patted me on the shoulder.

'I hope it doesn't come to it mate. Drive safely ok.'

I remember packing the important things that every bloke would appreciate; Playstation2, DVDs and a bag of clothes.

The journey was very memorable. I remember talking to her parents on my bluetooth earpiece, asking them to phone her as I had just left the house because she had asked for a divorce. They were in complete shock and a chain of phone calls began to take place. I was driving with my foot heavy on the accelerator. In the fast lane I was in tears driving over 100mph. I was undertaking cars that were not going fast enough. My thought was that I couldn't get to Somerset quick enough. I wanted to tell my Mother. I remember looking back at this moment thinking, what if the Police had stopped me? As I was an emotional wreck, would they have taken my driving licence off me, or would they have given me a break and given me a lift to Somerset, to get me there safely? If they had stopped me, it was likely I would have collapsed on to the floor and broken down in front of them. They'd probably have wondered why I was so emotional about getting stopped.

Have you ever thought about the songs of your life, the ones that stick in your mind relating to a particular moment in time. For me, this was one of those memorable moments. Driving to Somerset with one song on repeat. It's not a song I choose to listen to now. It's a Garth Brooks song titled 'Storm'. The chorus fitted the situation so well I remember singing the words at the top of my lungs as I drove like a looney along the M4 motorway.

> *'The door, it slammed like thunder*
> *and the tears they fell like rain*
> *and the warnings from her family*
> *whirl like a hurricane,*
> *she's drowning in emotions*
> *and she cannot reach the shore*
> *she's alive but can she survive the storm?'*
> **Garth Brooks 'The Storm'**

Isn't it funny how songs stick to a moment in time. Another I don't choose to listen to is the song we chose for the first dance at our wedding. In fact I struggle to listen to any of his songs now and that's Robbie Williams and the song titled 'She's The One'.

Telling my Mother wasn't easy. The once tough guy was now seeking his Mother's shoulder to cry on. I used to go to bed sobbing. It took a few weeks for this to pass. Once I'd got over the shock I was filling out the divorce papers with my legal adviser. This was stamped and the process started on the 19th July 2003.

Phone calls were exchanged frequently between Tina and I, but I wanted to keep things simple, clean cut and up front. She was using solicitors to deal with her stuff, but whoever was advising her was a complete amateur, trying to screw me down for money I never had. I remember telling her to stop wasting her money, as everything would be 50/50 and nothing else. The sale of the house needed to happen in order to pay for things and cover any debts we had as a couple. This went on for months but I stuck to my guns, no more, no less, 50/50 was what she was entitled to. She wanted to buy my share of the house to continue living there. She wasn't amused when I wanted half of the market share. She couldn't raise the funds and so ended up having to move out when the house was sold.

When the summer had passed I found a job working with adults with learning difficulties. This was a job I enjoyed doing and it gave me enjoyable job satisfaction. I was helping those who needed daily support with basic living skills. Anyhow, there was this lad who I was the Key Support worker to, who couldn't talk. His only form of communication was sign language, but this only worked when he was calm. If he became angry or agitated about something, the initial reaction was to ignore you. If anyone got too close to him, he'd lash out and his long arms would shoot out towards you to scratch you. Sometimes you had no warning that he wasn't feeling too good. After any struggles to stop him, he would calm down and we would encourage him to start using sign again. It was always good to see him sign 'sorry' and hug the staff afterwards. After one of these minor incidents, one staff member looked at me and said 'Neil, you're bleeding'.

I went off to look in the mirror. Where my polo shirt opened at the neck, his hand had got in there and three of his fingernails had scraped down towards my chest. Cleaning with antiseptic wipes made those wounds sting rather a lot, but it was something that needed to be done, and thoroughly. What these guys pick or poke even with the staff seeing is not worth mentioning here, but it sure would not be clean fingers, lets put it that way.

A couple of weeks had passed and I looked in the mirror to see the wounds on my chest not healing too well. I was a bit concerned that they had some sort of infection. I wasn't a lover of the doctors and let this go on for another couple of weeks. Why is it, some of the biggest, toughest, men are afraid of doctors and dentists? Needle phobia was high on my list of daft fears, yet a brawl in a street didn't faze me. Weird. However the doctor was needed, I had let the chest injury go on long enough. It was not only that, I also had a strange rash that was not clearing and was horribly itchy. It started on my wrists and ankles but was now beginning to spread across the lower back and had even spread to the nether-region. This rash was spreading fast. I was hoping that the Doc would give me some dermatological cream that would gradually ease the itchiness and clear the rash up. It didn't worry me, what worried me more was the visit to the surgery. I sat in the waiting room and the sweaty palms started. I saw my name digitally appear on the LED display. I was called to see a Doctor Cervelli. Typical, out of all the wholesome good English surnames like Roberts and Clarke I ended up with some foreigner who was in the UK and practising on us gullible British lot. Purely my view on the matter, you understand.

I walked into the room and said straightaway 'I'm not a fan of doctors so lets do this as quick as possibly, I've got this rash.'

He stopped me in my flow and invited me to take a seat.

'So where's this rash?'

I reluctantly went on. 'I've got it on my ankles and my wrists, it's also on my lower back and I'm embarrassed to say, on the bits that matter'.

Now I have come to the conclusion the Doctor was just in this to wind me up. 'Can you show me please?'

After a brief examination, the doctor took off his gloves and sat himself down at his desk, gesturing towards me to also return to my seat. He started telling me that he knew exactly what this was, and he began telling me the diagnosis. 'What you have sir is what is called 'Lichen Planus'. It is an inflammatory disease that affects the skin and the oral mucosa, and presents itself in the form of papules lesions or rashes. Basically, it's small red bumps that are shiny and flat to look at and vary in size from a pinhead to a centimetre across'.

I was cool with that, I knew I had red bumps and the name of it to me was immaterial. 'So there's a lotion or potion you can prescribe to stop this itching yeah?' What he said next shocked me to the point that I thought, what else could really go wrong in my life.

'I'm afraid not. At this stage there is nothing I can do for you. There is no cure for this disease. It can last for a period of six months or last up to about two years. It will undoubtedly get worse than what it already is. When the itchiness becomes unbearable, come and see me again because there is a steroid cream, but at this stage I wouldn't recommend it. With continuous use it thins the skin. It doesn't reduce the rash but can reduce the itchy feeling'.

Well, I ended up walking out of the surgery and back to the car. Before I even got to the car I began crying. I had some kind of long-term skin condition that was going to get worse. The things that went around my head were, where he had told me of all the other parts of the body that could be affected by this condition.

The mouth would potentially come up in ulcers, on the tongue and inner cheek areas. There was a possible stage of hair loss that may never grow back. The nails could become damaged and if they fell off, the damage was potentially permanent and they may never grow back. It could continue to spread across the body and the itchiness would never ease.

Great, so if you can imagine this big guy sat in the car for about ten minutes crying to himself and thinking, what else could happen to him in 2003?

I physically felt weak. I shouldn't have driven. If you want a scary visit on the Google website, type in Lichen Planus and see what pops up. When I started to read this at the time, I thought what is it that I have?

One evening I was driving along Burnham seafront and the phone went. Tina was on the other end ranting about something to do with the house and I started to feel angry at the constant harassing I was getting from her about money. I told her that money, divorce papers and house selling was not at the top of my agenda right now and she had no clue what was going on in my life and her continuous harassment was not helping matters. I told her I had been to the doctors and was diagnosed with a skin condition that could last up to two years. The silence at the end of the phone was broken after a slight pause when Tina asked.

'Are you ok?'

In a rapid response I replied 'Like you care, all you're interested in is money, you have no idea how I'm feeling right now and why should you care.'

I hung up. This was the last time I spoke to her until the post arrived on the 13th November 2003.

The divorce papers went through and came back from the County Court with a 'Decree Nisi' with a notice of six weeks for the 'Final Decree'. Work it out and you'll see I had an unfortunate Christmas present. Nice. You can't make this stuff up. Usually I go all out at Christmas and express joy and fun when visiting friends and family, but this was going to be a tough Christmas and one I'd remember for many years.

My skin cleared up after a few months thankfully. But it wasn't a breeze. The rash spread to most areas and was extremely irritating. I had mouth ulcers and my fingernails deteriorated. Itching for a week or two is enough but imagine it going on for months, it was no fun I tell you, but it did pass. I had visual marks left behind where the rash was, but it was no longer sore.

Since being back, I sought out a new circle of friends. I was looking to get in to the tough guy circle in Bridgwater. I caught up with a friend of mine who until now shielded me from his connections with the rougher crowd. But I was older now and could make my own choices. Two known brothers I was hanging out with for the next couple of years were loyal and tough. I'd made myself welcome in their homes and with their families. But if you got on the wrong side of them, they were always happy to help each other out when it came to aggro.

Bridgwater is a close community and locals would know of known names with a reputation for being trouble. I remember a time in my late teens when I was out drinking. I was sat in a bar in town, for those who are local it was the Rose and Crown in St Mary's Street. It was in the late nineties and one of the busier pubs in town on a Friday or Saturday night. I was sat with my mates and I spotted a chap walk in with a small crowd. As he walked in I was looking over at them and then turned to my mate to say something. Completely random, I don't remember talking about anything to do with him, but that didn't stop him coming over to me and having a go at me.

'Who do you think you're staring at, aye? If I catch your eyes in my direction again I'll come over here and knock you out, got it!'

I nodded with a puzzled feeling as to what had just occurred. I turned to my mate again and said to him 'Did you hear that guy?'

'What've you done Neil?' he said.

'I dunno?' I said and looked back over to the guy, he was looking back at me with a glare. I then saw a guy tap him on his shoulder and head-locked him in close to the guys head. Talking in his ear the guy looked over at me and nodded? I had no idea what was being said and I was beginning to brick it. I turned back to my mate. He was banging on about something to one of the others. With a bit of trouble I interrupted him and said, 'Now might be a good time to think about drinking up.'

'Hey pal!' This guy had only walked back over to me, for a split second I thought my heart stopped. I thought I was going to get dragged outside when he surprised me.

'Sorry pal, I didn't know who you were.'

Eh? I thought. He went on.

'I didn't realise you were one of the Tuckers, sorry mate, really I am.'

Hmmm... what had just occurred was even more of a puzzle. This was the first time I realised who my family were. My cousins were known and the family link had saved me. My cousins were the heavies in the town during the early nineties. I had a guy quivering without even realising I did anything. I remember speaking to one of my cousins soon after this encounter and they said exactly this.

'If you get in to any trouble whatsoever, get in touch and we'll sort it for you.' This was useful, and it gave me a sense of confidence when out on the town.

So with that, the work in Southampton, then onto Bridgwater mixing with the lads I was with, my life had been linked with heavies for some time now. These brothers were of the same league and known in the town for being a bit feisty. A baseball bat was part of their weaponry and a pair of concrete fists. These guys were solid lads. With the background of the doors, I felt comfortable around them and the adrenalin of the occasional bit of trouble excited me. I'd got in with a good pair of lads here and was beginning to feel at home.

These brothers lived close to each other. One day some loud mouth was hurling abuse outside Pete's house. Alex headed for the window and said that Pete, his brother was having a go, so we both headed for the door. When we got outside, Pete was stood there with his arms wide inviting them for a ruck saying, 'Shut your trap and get over here and have a go then!' There were three guys stood in the road looking like they were the business, until Alex stood next to him.

'What do these muppets want Pete?' Alex said.

'Well they keep saying they're going to have me, so I'm offering them to have a go, but they don't seem to want to now, they keep walking away'.

They were continuing to hurl abuse at him, but seeing Alex and I turn up, the other chaps were starting to realise it was now one on one and all was now even. The thing was, these were lads in their early twenties and we had the age and size advantage. All three of us were big and thug looking. Against these twenty something college boys, they were probably concerned that their good looks were about to be adjusted.

This wasn't the only bit of aggro that the brothers attracted, but if it ever happened I was there for the crack. They needed no encouragement from me, people used to just irritate them. One guy once walked past Alex's house and began to rattle a stick along his fence. Click, click, click, click, click, went the stick. Alex was sat in his front room and saw the guy through the window. He chucked the remote on the sofa with some force and headed for the door. 'Oi ****! Carry on and I'll knock you out pal!'

Click.

'IT AIN'T AS
GLAMOUROUS
AS IT
SOUNDS,
TRUST ME'

III. Other terms to be obs...

This agreement shall be binding u...
representativ... Time is of th...esse...
enforced u..der the laws of the S...

This is the entire agree...

Sign...ed ...ar first writte...

Signed in the presenc...e of:

First Party:

Second Party:

APPROVED

TRACT

CONFIDENTIAL

'IT AIN'T AS GLAMOUROUS AS IT SOUNDS, TRUST ME' 08

Alex was out of that front door quicker than a Yorkshire terrier. He slammed the gate open and the poor lad must have been thinking, 'What's his problem?'

Whack, and the lad ended up on the floor. This is a short example of what occurred in their world. But I trusted them, they trusted me, and we had a great friendship. Whenever there was a chance for a ruck I was there ready for it to go off.

When you read most doorman biographies you read about the doorman who has gone bad and been put in prison for their thuggish approach to their work. Or, you read about the doorman who gets into the foreign security industry, offering muscle where needed and getting paid silly money to bodyguard or carry fire arms, acting undercover. You hear of tales where they see their friends killed whilst stood next to them, from a stab wound or a bullet. What makes me laugh is when you hear that in one book, Manchester has some of the most violent gangs in the country, then in the next book it's East End London, another in the Midlands etc etc and it goes on. For me, it's anywhere. Wherever you live it's bad and we all have our own reputations. I remember Bridgwater as having a foul reputation in the late 1980's and early 1990's. Bristol lads would come to Bridgwater for a night out because they knew a fight would break out. The local rag would report stories like, 'Man dies in a club from a machete' or 'Man dies after being stabbed'. These stories were beginning to get more and more popular. Bridgwater lads would start going to Bristol to do exactly the same to have a great night out. In Bridgwater, a ruck was part of the experience of a night out. I remember catching up with some mates from Bristol, from my youth days at the YMCA. As pub goers they often heard rumours that Bridgwater was not a place to go for a night out, because if you said you were from Bristol, you were likely to get your head kicked in, which was an interesting insight.

In the late 1980's, we never had wide news coverage on this sort of stuff, so regional news would always milk the story to the point where they expressed the view that the said locality was becoming the worst in the country for violence. Well maybe this did happen, but I fear more and more that most areas are coming to the brink of violent outbreaks on a weekly basis. If you look at the statistics on the subject of violent crime in local areas, Manchester currently is very low in comparison to other areas in the country. That's not saying violent crime is decreasing, if anything it is on the increase, but Manchester is not a known hotspot for trouble on a night out.

Off the soap box, I often thought how easy it may be to further the security work I had gained experience in and thought that anything could be achieved if really desired. Plough money into any training and you'd get a job abroad in some security position.

I was chatting to my legal adviser who one day asked me to think about pursuing a new career. A self-employed opportunity was arising and he was asking me to seriously consider what he was saying. This was a combination of skills and experience from my past employment and training all in one job. Sounded interesting.

'We often hire these in, and if you can offer it slightly cheaper, we'll be able to put work your way' he said.

The job my friend was asking me to consider was as a private investigator. The services of the job included process serving, injury investigations and legal services to the solicitors offices. This sounded like a minefield of training and a business full of litigation and red tape. I spoke to the legal chap and suggested a partnership with Alex who had amazing local knowledge. I also wanted the legal advisor to consider partnering silently, to provide continuous support and advice. He agreed and said that he'd help in any way he could with advice but couldn't get involved in any of the hands on stuff. Within a month this was set up. I had a bank account sorted and an office rented for the job. An office address was important. I couldn't have any repercussions coming to a home address. I dealt with the marketing and publicity locally and began getting the jobs in. The business name was GNA Private Investigators and it was established in March 2004. The Security Industries Act was taking their time to put licensing measures in place for the investigators, who were debating about the level of security information they were entitled to and how much a suitable licence would cost. This meant setting up the business at this point was relatively easy. I enquired about suitable training and paid the fees to gain a qualification, to support the day when licensing came in. I found out that one of the main jobs for the investigator was to trace and locate individuals, then issue them with a court summons, known as a 'Process Serve'.

Process Serving was one of the first jobs that came in. Some poor chap was in major debt and a court summons needed issuing. I found the property and the nerves were starting to kick in. What would happen? I wouldn't be a welcome visitor to anyone when they received a summons to attend court. My job was to record the serve as accurately as possible, because if needed, I may have to attend court to state for the record that I issued a summons on the said person, at the said location, at a said time. I remember knocking on his door and this little kid answering. He was silent as he opened the door.

'Is your Dad in?' I said.

'Yeah' this kid said.

'Can you tell him it's Neil at the door for him?'

'Yeah' and he ran off.

The door was left wide open. The chap came to the door and I introduced myself as being appointed by the acting solicitors and needed to present him with the court summons. He took the document off me, thanked me and closed the door politely. I knew not all of these jobs would be like this, but it was a welcome start. If they were all like this it'd be easy.

But they weren't and I was about to get some process serving jobs that were a bit tougher. There was one in particular where I feared for my own safety. He refused to accept the document I was serving upon him, but it didn't work like that, I remember throwing the summons at him so it hit his chest. As it fell to the floor, I remember saying to him.

'You don't have a choice Mr Nelson, that's just been served'.

As I walked back to the car I signalled silently to my driver to start the engine. As I got in, I said 'Let's get out of here, he wasn't too happy with that one'. We reversed out of the farm like a scene from a 1970's cop drama.

Not all cases were simple postman jobs some were helpful for the clients. One chap was approaching sixty and had been adopted into a family at birth, having never met his biological Mother. His family had done some of the legwork researching names but had no clue as to how to get started on a nationwide search. A simple database search was carried out and I'd come up with four possible locations. When these were presented to the client, he knew straight away that one of the addresses was one of the previous locations known to the family and was a likely success. We were instructed to make a personal visit to speak to the now elderly woman who was given the opportunity to meet with her estranged son who she never got to see grow up. If this would not be an option, we could at least open an opportunity to write to them and start communications after many years. Jobs like this made the work worthwhile.

As the work began coming in, I was finding that we were getting numerous calls about cheating husbands, from women who had suspicious minds. All of these cases hinted at the men arriving home from work late and not being contactable by phone. One case in particular required us to follow a bloke from his workplace. I'll be vague about the details, but what was humorous about this one in particular was the fact that this guy borrowed a vehicle from another work colleague. The bloke had borrowed a Porsche, but we identified him easy enough. Even though he couldn't have had a clue about us, he knew how to drive this thing because he left us standing. Speeding off into the distance, we ended up phoning the client to tell her we had lost him and that we'd have to try another day. We worked out that the guy had used a crafty shortcut to the motorway services and sped off up the motorway. This supported her suspicion that he had a bit on the side near Bristol. It was a short investigation and surveillance job, which only came up with one nugget. However, that was enough for her at that stage to start asking questions about trust in their relationship.

I was finding that we were regularly providing information to support clients and their argument for divorce proceedings. Here was I, a divorcee, helping others get the divorce they desired.

It wasn't always supporting a case for a divorce. One time a chap came to us to keep an eye on his mistress. He was a married man, having an affair and he wanted us to check that the woman, who he was prepared to leave his marriage for, wasn't cheating on him with someone else. As bizarre as this sounds, it took two days to get one photo. We'd followed this woman, who was accompanied by an unidentified male, to a restaurant where we needed to get a photo. I entered the restaurant and asked to speak to the manager. I explained my purpose for the visit and that I could do with their help to get a photo, without looking too suspicious walking into a restaurant with a digital camera. They were up for helping and were prepared to assist inside. The set-up was that I was posing as a newspaper photographer and needed a promotional shot of the manager showing some menus in their hand. The idea was that the manager would stand in a certain position, in order that I could take a shot over his shoulder of the woman and her male friend enjoying a glass of wine and a meal together.

As I left the premises with the money shot, I left through the quickest exit I could find by walking through the kitchen, at the shock of the chef, who followed me out challenging me.

'Who the hell do you think you are? Who are you?'

I continued to walk to the van.

My driver asked, 'Got it?'

'Yep superb shot!' I replied, checking the camera display for the pictures. The client was paying several hundred pounds for this one photo. The video camera surveillance of the woman's home was a bonus, but not as compounding as the photo. We presented our findings reports in a very high standard of presentation and the client was extremely pleased with our service.   On this occasion our work resulted in saving a marriage.

Let me take a short moment to describe our main surveillance vehicle to you. It had two tiny hidden wired cameras facing the front and back of the vehicle. We would use a normal camcorder for the zoom function needs. These three cameras were wired to a signal splitter and then linked to a laptop in order to record the footage digitally. Another laptop recorder was for audio. In one of the vehicle's external air vents was a highly sensitive microphone that could pick up conversations from tens of metres away. This was in one of those rotating air vents that would usually spin in the wind, but this was used as a directional microphone. Industry regulations stated that the use of cameras was permitted, but when it recorded audio using covert technology a license was needed, this kind of license was held by CID officers and MI5 agents, not some small timer in Bridgwater with a small van on a matrimonial case.

In all honesty, this was a Mickey Mouse set up, but it worked, and it worked well. No audio was ever recorded because it would be dismissible in court, but it was used when necessary to help with the investigations, albeit unofficially. The interior of the van was panelled out with wood and then covered in carpet for some warmth on those cold nights. I had a fridge plugged in there too, for those thirst and hunger needs. In a cupboard I had various items of clothing for quick disguises, such as a workman, in jeans and fleece or a set of overalls and a hard hat. There were also other useful bits of equipment like high-powered torches. A real gadget van that any geek could only dream of.

We once got a job in from a business that was having difficulty with a customer paying for services carried out. This was a tree surgeon who had carried out some work in a conservation area. The cuts made to the tree were applied for to the local council and the cuts authorised were carried out. However, the customer didn't agree that the work carried out was according to the instructions agreed. Our client was forming a case for the small claims process, for debt collection. Our work was to gain access to the property and gain photographs of the completed work for evidence to support the small claim proceedings. Alex couldn't join me on this one, so I had asked my Father to be the driver for this job. We arrived at the address and found the owner out, but his garden maintenance chap working in the front garden of the property.

'Excuse me, are you Mr Patrick?'

'No, he's out at the moment, I'm his gardener, can I help you?'

We were talking to him through a six-foot high metal gate. I passed him a card, introduced ourselves and asked if we could see the tree in question, which was situated at the rear of the garden. He obliged and allowed us onto the property.

'Yeah, no problems gents two secs, I'll get the gates opened for you.'

This was an easy one. It was great when people were helpful in giving the evidence. The metal gates electronically opened and the gardener was heard on the intercom.

'Come on in gents.'

We walked on in, meeting the gardener by the main entrance to the building. He led us to the back of the property. We were shown the tree with the work done on it and I took the necessary pictures. As our clients had told us, it was clear work had been carried out on the tree. Our job was to make sure we had pictures to show this clearly. After identifying the tree, we then needed shots taken from the other side. We left the property and proceeded to go to the back of the property for our remaining couple of photos. Once done we began walking back to our vehicle.

'That wasn't too bad, even easier when the gardener invites you in to get the photo you need!' my Dad said.

As he said this, the owner of the property came around the corner. I thought to myself, here we go lets have the aggro. I told my Father to get in the vehicle and start the engine ready to leave, but the guy surprised me. I think he was prepared for the evidence gathering as he felt he had a strong case against the charges for what he considered was unfinished work. He was as helpful as the gardener. We exchanged details and on the return to the office, I began some negotiations over the phone to try and bring a resolution to the outstanding bill.

It doesn't matter whether you agree with the work of the investigator or not. In court solicitors need evidence to support a case and that is the investigators job. It was not at all glamorous and didn't involve fast cars or fast women. You end up keeping the job a secret from anyone local, apart from close family. You sit in the back of a van for hours watching nothing and recording any movement in and around a subject's property. You even get to identify the neighbour's cat and start noticing the weird habits of the neighbours love for their gardens. It can be funny to watch, but most of the time it can be quite a boring job. The use of gadgets helped to keep my mind active.

I had some finances left over from the divorce and the house sale, which I invested into the business, purchasing equipment and furniture. Although work was coming in, it wasn't enough to keep my expenses going, so I had to find alternative employment. This is where the YMCA came to my aid. A friend of mine who worked there had a Housing Support Officer job going. It was overnight, which was ideal. I could do my investigation work and get some sleep before going in to start work there at 11pm. During the night I could type up my investigator reports and have the office work done at night, getting paid to do both. My finances were beginning to pick up slowly and I was starting to stay afloat. It was only a part time job, which meant that social time was still possible.

My social life up until now had suffered, because I wasn't very good company. I felt a spare part with couples around me. However, I soon got to the point where I realised I didn't miss Tina. Bizarre to say it, but it was true. I was finding I kept myself so busy, that burning the candle at both ends helped to keep my mind off the emotional stuff. I caught up with a few old pals and began building a good social network.

I'd bought an old Mitsubishi 4x4 motor for the main purpose of green laning. This is where you can take the road worthy vehicle on tracks that are impossible for the conventional car to venture down. Sometimes these tracks had become overgrown to the point that even horses couldn't walk along them. These tracks were on the ordinance survey maps as byways for vehicles, similar to a footpath but for cars, so you got to see a different side to the countryside. To preserve them, because of the increase in use for family days out, the local governments had gradually blocked these off. Walkers and horse riders would complain that the countryside was being destroyed by the presence of vehicles, we'd argue that unless you wanted to take a machete with you on your walks out in the countryside, the vehicles could have done the job. Instead these lanes would most likely overgrow with plant life, never be used and eventually be forgotten about.

After this blow to the social outings with fellow offroaders, we hunted out the club circuit for offroaders known as the All Wheel Drive Club. The local group met on the last Sunday of every month for track competitions. We could still get our adrenaline fix, but in a more authorised way. It made sense and made it competitive, everything a man wants. It was a chance to drive at peculiar angles and on occasions tip over, coming home with numerous bruises and scrapes. I added some sticker work to the bonnet and emptied out the vehicle of all the unnecessary furnishings. This was now a two-seater beaten up 4x4, still taxed and roadworthy well at least until the next MOT.

The guys who were part of the offroading group were a fun bunch and the increase in friends meant I had more coffee locations in and around Bridgwater. I would spend a fair bit of time meeting up with folks drinking coffee and enjoying a few biscuits. It was these times where I'd get most of the PI work, from referrals from friends.

'LOYALTIES OF PAST FRIENDSHIPS MEANT NOTHING'

'LOYALTIES OF PAST FRIENDSHIPS MEANT NOTHING'

If you met a Private Investigator for the first time what would you think? Would you think 'yeah whatever it's just a job.' Most likely not, most people I met all reacted in a similar way. First, they'd be surprised that the person they knew had this kind of job, and second, they'd want in on the action. People used to say, 'Oh I'd love to do that job!'. I always replied by saying 'It sounds a good job until you get to do it. You end up sitting for hours watching a home, sometimes for no evidence, because without realising it the people were not in,' or 'It isn't as glamorous as it sounds, trust me.'

I'd gone through the summer of 2004 and was now approaching the silly season for Bridgwater. For the locals our calendar started in September. We had our local travelling fair at the end of September, carnival concerts at the town hall in October and then Europe's largest illuminated carnival procession in November, after this the Christmas décor started. Time flew by in Somerset at this end of the year.

It was early September and my Dad phoned me with some news that shook the family. No family wants to hear of a death, but they definitely don't want to hear that a relative has died as a result of being attacked.

When I went to work on the day the story appeared in the local paper, a work colleague came up to me and asked if the named person was a relative. They showed true compassion towards me at first. They then apologised for what I was about to hear.

'The lad that did it Neil, is my daughter's boyfriend.'

The rage inside was starting to rise. She went on to say, 'This is totally out of character, he says it was an accident and the man fell and hit his head on the railings.'

I couldn't talk to her. I was speechless. I didn't know what to say to her. The initial response in my mind was, now I know how to find him I'll send the lads round for a visit.

'The law is an ass' was a common saying around this topic for some time. We closely watched the case news and attended court to hear first hand what the outcome was. The death of my relative was plastered across the local newspapers and the name of the attacker was dragged about the news for months afterwards. He was sent to prison for manslaughter. As it was an accidental death this guy was only given a 4 year sentence, which meant in the real world, he was likely to be out within 2 years for killing someone.

My grandparents were totally shocked by the news and found the whole thing extremely upsetting. It was an outrageous act by the attacker, who was in his early twenties and had attacked a man in his late sixties, after his recent retirement. The sentence frustrated them even more and they couldn't believe that this was what the judge deemed appropriate for the death of their family member. At times like this it's difficult to accept it, but life goes on.

The manager of an entertainments firm contacted GNA for some advice. He told me that one of his fairground amusements was on its way to the 2004 Bridgwater Fair. He explained his enquiry and asked for our assistance. A corporate client, who was not short of a few bucks, would more than likely pay well, so this had great potential. Unfortunately, my partners could not assist with the work, as they were both now in full time employment. I was finding that I was taking this work on, but had no one to help me. This job required constant surveillance but how was I going to do this on my own?

'My Son-in-law is fiddling the books,' said Mr Thompson.

He was the Father of the entertainment business and had his family out on the road with various amusements. He co-ordinated the bookings in the diary for them to travel from place to place.

'I'm concerned he's taking on extra bookings and using my equipment for his own pocket. When he sends in the figures for the regular bookings they're down, but not by a little, it's down a few grand. This is happening everywhere he's going, my others on the road are experiencing a slow down in takings, but this is just flagging up because it's too obvious. Thing is, I need the evidence to catch him at it. I want to know the number of rides and the tariff he's showing.'

I thought this was quite a meaty task. I needed up-close photos and to count every time the ride started up, without getting caught. If I got noticed, or on their nerves, I knew this travelling fair lot would stick together. I could see myself getting done over good and proper. The reputation of these people was to punch first and don't even bother asking questions later. How was I going to stick around in a closely packed fairground for four days, without being noticed? I was keen to take on the work though.

'We can get the evidence you need Mr Thompson, let me start a case file for you and take some further details down.'

The background of the case was that the Father was looking for a reason to get shut of the Son-in-law. The fact that he was creaming off the cash was a good way to do it. Mr Thompson's daughter was having relationship problems with her husband and he was doing his little bit to add fuel to the fire, for a satisfactory divorce as an outcome. He wanted to get the guy out using a legal route, to help the daughter when it came to the legal proceedings to get rid of him. It's funny, but whatever I got work wise, it was always matrimonial one way or another. Even so, the primary concern here was tax fraud. I had to record his activities and Mr Thompson would check what came in at his end.

I spent four days at the fairground, taking numerous photos

and recording the number of rides. I had to move from my observation point, because the old boy on the dodgems was keeping his eye on me. When I moved away he was watching where I was going. Not a nice feeling, I was just hoping that it wasn't too obvious who I was. These were long nights, especially having to do it alone, but in general, all went ok. I'd got through the investigation recording everything that was needed. At the end of it I sent off the findings report with supporting evidence of photos.

Mr Thompson called me up three weeks later, telling me that the supporting evidence helped to send the guy packing and the legal proceedings were starting. However, my presence at the fair didn't go unnoticed and the Son-in-law knew he was being watched, but thought I was an Inland Revenue investigator, which really rattled him. So the impact and pressure from the Father was useful in getting him out of the family. So all was well in the Thompson household again.

I remember thinking, home ain't what it cracked up to be and I was slotting back into the old ways from before I left the town. The experience I'd gained and lifestyle I had was out of the window. Have you ever moved away from your hometown and returned a year or two later? Did you notice that nothing changes and life goes on regardless of where you have been and what you have got up to? For me, I found my return to Bridgwater a bit annoying. I had done so much and gained so much confidence away from this potsy little town, but no one seemed to have noticed.

One of my mates who I had grown up with, had his own business now, but in his social life hadn't changed one bit. His life involved drinking, socialising and chatting up the ladies. For me, I couldn't take this any more. The way he'd treat them annoyed me. In the older days I wouldn't have said anything, but I had changed. I was a different kind of guy now. It was seven years later and a lot had happened in seven years. The final straw was a mix up with my mate Alex. This friend had upset him somehow and I'd chosen to support Alex. My loyalties of a past friendship meant nothing. I was sticking with a new friend who I felt had a good argument. I told this guy I'd had enough and that our friendship would no longer be what it used to be. I wouldn't bad mouth him to anyone, he was good at what he did, but we'd no longer be the buddies we were in my late teens and early twenties. This longstanding friendship was now over.

Alex and Pete were part of the offroading group of lads who met up regularly and I had found a comfort zone that was filling the need for an adrenaline kick every now and again. I still spent most of my spare time with these guys. The offroad motor sport was picking up and my interest in the competitiveness of the sport was beginning to increase. Every month I would turn up hoping to give my fellow drivers a run for their money. However, it never worked out as well as this, and I'd usually be bringing up the rear in terms of points. I'd saved up some cash and bought some new tyres for the job, these were called grizzly claws and made a huge difference to the game. Within a couple of months this brought me up to the middle of the league and made me more of a threat to the other lads on the competition days. In this sport it was all hands on to turn over rolled vehicles. Although I never rolled completely I did end up on my side on one occasion. A muddy day out, but a laugh a minute nonetheless. I had a successful web site packed full of photos and the top scores from the day that had hundreds of visits per month.

I got another surveillance job in, again another matrimonial case. This one was to support custody of the kids. It was horrible stuff to get into. How can solicitors take on a case knowing it's supporting the wrong side? How do they justify it in their own minds to take the case on. I'm not saying I supported the wrong side, I just believe there are two sides to every story.

I had to carry out a weeks worth of surveillance to provide evidence for my client's solicitor, supporting the case that the client's partner was co-habiting with another person. No problem. The location was good, I could get a good enough observation point from far enough away and my zoom lenses on the stills camera would be good enough. For the sake of being unnoticed and obvious, I asked my Father to be a driver for this job.

'Yes of course son, I've got those shifts off work this week.'

My Father worked for the local mental health, but was always interested in lending a hand. This was to be a good partnership for the next few days.

Before getting to the observation point, I'd get out of the van, step into the back of it and get my Father to drive the vehicle to the observation point. He would park up and leave the location on foot, leaving me in the back of the vehicle, for a duration, to spot the two subjects leaving the property for work. Thing was, their work hours meant we had to be in position early in the morning. We had to be in position at 4.45am every morning, because they left for work about an hour later.

'Here?' My Father would ask as he lined the vehicle up to the best point for the cameras to observe the house.

'Forward a bit … yep that's it!'

'Right son, give me a call when your ready to be picked up and I'll come on back.'

'Cheers Dad, speak to you in a bit'

When the surveillance was done, I phoned my Father and he would return to the vehicle and drive off down the road.

'I spotted them myself up the road leaving I knew you'd call shortly afterwards,' said my Father.

A short distance down the road he stopped the van to let me out of the back at a safe location, unobserved by onlookers. This was an easy job and gathering the required evidence was easy.

On the last day of the surveillance, my Father couldn't drive for me neither could Alex, so I had to find another driver. I asked a friend of mine who worked for the YMCA to drive for me. This was an eye opener for them, to see me carry out the work I often talked to them about.

This was a fun surveillance and the results were very supportive for the client's case with their solicitors. The evidence we produced was the best the solicitors had ever seen. This was a good morale booster and a successful case result.

I was enjoying this work and finding that I was more often than not successful with each case that came up. It was amazing how easy it was. It wasn't intelligence that got results, more often than not it was patience. If you got inpatient and irritable, you'd get noticed or uncover nothing because you couldn't stick around long enough to get the information you were after.

What was funny was that on days where I walked into my night job wearing a suit, the residents at the YMCA were starting to wonder what I did during the day. As my experience in security work was increasing, I'd walk around with a sense of authority and confidence when wearing a suit. I still do it today. Ask any bloke. Put on a good suit and a decent pair of shoes and your exterior changes the way you feel inside. For me, I had a doorman feeling where nothing could faze me or harm me. So I walked around with that kind of attitude. It's funny how people notice this in someone. These residents were beginning to ask questions. They were fishing for information, which would disclose my day job. I remember the potential work the Housing Manager had previously mentioned to me. He said my services would be useful in the future, assisting with trace and locate jobs for residents who did a runner owing some rent to the organisation. So I wanted to keep my private life private from this bunch. But that didn't stop the questions.

Then the question of all questions, which led them down the garden path, which gave them something to go on was this.

'Can you arrest people?'

I immediately replied, 'Yes'.

This was enough for them. The two that came to ask ran off and were heard in the distance saying to each other, 'I told you he was CID, didn't I!' I laughed to myself. What made it even funnier was how quick this went around and how many believed it.

This rumour even travelled around locally where I lived and I had my neighbours (who were educationally challenged) calling out 'Oi are you filth?' or saying as I'd walk by 'He's old bill he is' to their mates. Hilarious.

When I purchased another motor, it was the best motor on the street, which raised questions with the locals who were cheeky enough to ask how much it cost. In their heads the CID sized salary supported the size and cost of the vehicle. It fit with the image they had created in their mind. As a kid, I used to watch the American action series called The Fall Guy. Colt Seavers, the bounty hunter and stunt man had a brown pick-up and he drove it on his bounty hunting cases. If you ask a kid what they want to be when they grow up, you might hear the words 'a doctor' or 'a pilot'. I would answer 'a stunt man'. My Mother would nod her head and confirm this to anyone and start telling them that I was on first name terms with the local hospital, because I had hurt myself or cut myself open on something. How my old bike survived the smashes and crashes I'll never know. But my body would fall from great heights and land on hard tarmac or concrete quite often. I was an action junkie as a kid and I loved the action junkie lifestyle that I had now I was older. But back to the motor, this was my dream motor. It was a 4x4 pickup style motor and one I had longed for, for some time.

November arrived and my Grandparents got a phone call from my Dad, who shared with them some more shocking news for the family. Another close relative was again a victim of a violent attack and was in hospital. This sent my Grandparents into another emotional roller coaster, which at their age they could do without.

This next chapter is the story that changed my world. I used to be proud of the fact that I could say in all of this violent and aggressive world I'd been a part of, that I'd never been punched, but on the 20th November 2004 that all changed.

"IT'S GONNA NEED SURGERY TO FIX THIS"

'IT'S GONNA NEED SURGERY TO FIX THIS' 10

At 9.45pm I arrived at work in my 4x4. Driving into the car park I noticed a bit of aggro between three individuals. I sat in the car for a short while as I watched them go on at each other. I then gathered my belongings. The three individuals were two males and one female. The three of them were in their mid to late teens. The verbal agro was between the two males and the female was holding one male back. The one being held back wanted to lump the other. The other male was being verbal but at any point where the first male could get away from the female, would run fearing he'd get a battering.

It was a wet night and the car park tarmac was glistening with the floodlights shining on it. The volume of the shouting was beginning to draw attention. This was looking like a familiar night on the doors. Behind most barneys was a girl who would scream at the top of her lungs and give the lad a reason for acting up, to show her that he could handle himself. It was usually bravado, all talk and no action. But it seemed the girls loved the attention and the involvement.

'Get out of my way! Let me have him!' said the guy, trying to get past the girl holding him back.

'No Liam, leave him alone' the girl screamed. She turned towards the other lad who was stood there, 'Just go!' As the guy turned and started walking out of the car park, the pursuing lad pushed passed the girl and followed him, the girl also followed. When all three had left the car park, I got out of the car and went into the main reception. As I walked in I saw an agency worker behind the reception.

'Did you see any of that outside?'

He responded with a puzzled look on his face 'Whas'at?'

'Domestic I guess, but the one with the attitude was a bit feisty'

At this point I had no clue who any of the three were.

Not even thinking to ask the unknowledgeable agency worker, I said to him, 'Who's on?' referring to the employed staff on site.

'Jeanette's in', he replied, as I walked down the corridor towards the housing office.

I walked into the office and saw Jeanette.

'Did you hear the shouting in the car park?' I said.

'No? Who is it?' she asked.

'I have no idea, but it didn't look too good.'

As I said this you could now hear the shouting from the back of the office. 'Can you hear them outside? They've walked off site now. There was a girl holding a guy back who was wanting to have a go with another lad, looks like they had just come out of here.'

'Let's have a look and see who it is.' She locked the office door and headed for the reception. I had left my stuff in the office and followed her. We stood in the reception watching the CCTV cameras. Within a minute or so a car entered the car park. A chap in his thirties, who was unknown to us, parked his car and walked out of the car park.

Another car entered the car park. It was the other night worker, Gary. He walked in to the reception and mentioned the disturbance just outside the car park.

'Aye there's something kicking off out there, are they our lot?' Jeanette asked 'Are they still at it then?'

'Yeah, didn't seem too friendly either' said Gary.

Whilst we were stood there chatting, the original three returned, along with the guy who pulled up in his car. As soon as Jeanette could see who they were she said, 'That's Liam Anderson and his girlfriend, he's a new resident here.'

The guy who had parked his car in the car park was now beginning to get involved and tried to hold Liam back from his original target. This allowed the scared lad to leg it away from Liam. In a split second Liam turned and targeted his aggression towards the man who helped the lad escape.

Jeanette then said, 'That's it! He can come inside and pack this in.' Jeanette pressed the release button on the electronic doors and headed out into the car park with myself. Gary and the Agency worker followed us as we walked towards the disturbance. As we walked out, Liam was beginning to chase the guy around a parked vehicle. As Liam would walk one way, the guy walked in the other direction. Liam was pacing aggressively around the car.

'Come here... Why are you walking away from me...? Come here... I'm going to sort you out !'

This all appears tame in the language and if you can picture the scenario you'll probably start hearing the aggressive language used. I'm sure you get the idea. As we got closer the aggressive manner was beginning to be felt and the tension was evident. This was potentially going to end up bad. As staff members, we had a duty of care for all involved, to try and calm the situation down and separate the individuals, avoiding any unnecessary trouble.

'Come on Liam, calm down and come inside aye?' said Jeanette.

Liam stopped pacing. He turned to Jeanette, leaned towards her raising a pointed arm and shouted 'Stay out of this, it ain't got any'fin to do wiv you, so back off!'

He turned around and began pacing around the car again pursuing the other guy. I'd positioned myself at the front of the parked car and as Liam approached me I also said the same as Jeanette. 'What's up, why not come inside and tell us what's upset you aye?'

With that, using both of his hands, he pushed hard to shift me out of his way. I wasn't expecting to be shoved and ended up taking steps backwards to regain my balance.

'What's it gotta do wiv you lot?' he said as he walked by continuing to pursue the other chap.

Jeanette called out to him as he continued pacing around the car. 'Liam, if you don't calm down we would have to call…' She didn't finish the sentence because Liam was shouting so loud towards the other guy. This guy looked scared and was continuing to keep his eyes on Liam, making sure he was avoiding him, by using the car as a safety barrier. As he started to approach me for the second time, I stood in a solid stance to avoid losing my balance again if he tried to push me again.

'Come on Liam, come on inside and calm down aye?' I said calmly.

He approached me quickly and pushed me with both his arms in the chest again and unprovoked he struck me with a solid uppercut to the lower jaw. It was a left-handed punch, which struck the right side of my jaw. I had never felt such a knock as this. It was an instant pain. My head rolled back and I turned my head to the right. The inside of my mouth felt weird. Without knowing it, I thought that I may have lost a tooth. Bare in mind this was all a bit slow motion, because what seemed like one second later, the second punch was on its way in. This was a right-handed punch, which made contact with the now exposed left side of my jaw.

Everything went dark as I closed my eyes and spun around due to the impact of the second punch. I pulled my hands up towards my face to protect it. With my back now towards him and still standing he got another chance to plant one on me. Bang. Jeanette turned around and started to run back to the reception.

'That's it I'm calling the Police' she said.

In came another solid punch, this time on the back of my skull. I opened my eyes and was about to say 'Someone get him off' when I saw Liam passing my left hand side. The agency worker trained in control and restraint had managed to grab hold of his left arm. I immediately knew that Liam had some strength and that the agency worker would not be able to take him down alone, so I grabbed hold of Liam's right arm. As soon as we both had the arm locks, we started to force his body towards the floor. As he fell to his knees we forced his shoulders into the floor. As soon as he was locked up I told him that he had assaulted a member of staff and that we were restraining him for Police arrest. My sensations were beginning to come back and my head was hurting, but the adrenaline had kicked in and my strength was holding on to this guy nice and tight. He wasn't moving anywhere.

As Liam went to the floor he landed on his knees. If you can picture it, kneel down and put your head to the floor with your hands behind your back. (If you're trying this in your room, it may help to sit back down again to keep reading, otherwise the next few chapters will be pretty uncomfortable!). This is how he was, but the agency worker and myself were holding his arms and forcing his shoulders onto the floor. Sometimes when you restrain violent characters you need a third person to keep the legs locked up as well. By kneeling down Liam had effectively locked them up for us, making it very easy to hold him safely on the floor, without any further risk of being hit or losing grip on the restraint.

Liam shouted out. 'Let me up, it hurts'

He was complaining that his cheek was being pressed into the tarmac of the car park. This was not considered to be a major concern but more of a ploy to have the restraint loosened. The restraint was not excessive and thankfully to the agency worker, appropriately carried out. I replied to him, realising that my mouth was hurting and struggling to talk properly.

'Like I give a rip!'

As I said this I spat out a mouthful of blood on to the tarmac. Looking down, I realised I was losing a lot of blood and that I needed to clean up. I turned around and saw the staff member Gary stood there.

'Come and hold onto him so I can check my injuries.'

I wouldn't loosen my grip until I knew Gary had a good hold of him. I backed out of the restraint and walked quickly to the main reception. As I walked in I saw Jeanette by the reception using the phone. I heard her tell the emergency services that a staff member had been assaulted and we needed immediate assistance. I walked into the gent's toilets and looked in the mirror. It hurt to open my mouth and the swelling was starting to appear. It looked like my jaw was to one side, and I thought that due to the amount of pain, I may have had a dislocated jaw. I grabbed some tissue paper from the cubicle and wiped my chin carefully of the blood. I walked back into the reception. Glancing outside towards the staff restraining Liam, I noticed that they were experiencing some difficulty holding Liam because the girlfriend was trying to release him by grabbing Gary's arm. As I saw this I walked straight back out there and grabbed the girl by the right arm, putting this into an arm lock. I pulled her away from Gary and walked her over to the nearest vehicle, pushing her on to the boot of the car. The girl was screaming, which to me seemed a bit excessive.

'Get off my arms, my arms!'

The guy who drove in and was being pursued by Liam assisted with this restraint and explained to me who he was.

'Alright alright, ease off her mate, I'll deal with her, I'm a staff member of Oak Lodge and she's one of ours.'

Oak Lodge was a young people's care home.

'She's got cuts on her arms, let go of her!' he continued.

'Liam is going to be arrested, we could do with not letting him go, so keep her out of the way! Alright!' I said.

As I left him to sort her out, I looked back at Gary and the agency worker who were now having further trouble with another onlooker. He was shouting at them to release the restrained Liam.

'Let him go you b******s!' He shouted.

I walked towards the lad, scooped him up with my arm and pulled him away.

'The staff are restraining him to be arrested by the police, I'd appreciate it if you back off!'

As I was stood in front of him blocking his sight of Liam, he looked over at the female and called out to her.

'You alright?'

As I raised my arm to gesture to him to walk away, he fell over and yelled in pain claiming I'd hit him. This was turning into a comedy. I stood there wondering why this guy wanted in on the action?

'You carry on you muppet, I'm not playing your games' and I turned around. This was getting way too much attention. Another female turned up and starting showing some concern for Liam. As I looked towards the restraining staff members, I saw a Police unit turn up. The vehicle came speeding into the car park and pulled up next to us. Two police officers jumped out, one male officer, one female. They relieved the staff of the restraint and looked up at me.

'Why is this person under restraint?'

I explained to the officers 'As staff we were alerted to a problem here in the car park. Trying to calm down a situation, he turned on me and punched me. He is restrained ready to be arrested for assault.'

'Ok, I'm placing you under arrest for grievous bodily harm. You do not have to say anything, but it may harm your defence if you do not mention, when questioned, something which you later rely on in court. Anything you do say may be given in evidence.'

With that the officer placed the handcuffs on him and pulled him up to his feet. The girlfriend from Oak Lodge came over to him and kissed him. The female officer pulled the girl to one side leaving the male officer holding one arm. I went to the other arm and assisted the Police officer in putting Liam into the caged section of the van. Another Police Unit arrived and assisted with bringing the situation to some normality.

I walked into the main building and one of the arresting officers came over to me, asking if I was ok. To be honest I was in immense pain and by now could hardly open my mouth to talk. The female officer then asked me for my name and address. I tried talking but winced in pain.

'I'm sorry I can see it's painful to talk do you want to write it down for me?' Even better idea, I pulled my card wallet out of my pocket and produced my driving licence card with it all on.

'That's a good idea', she said. 'Do you want to sit down?' was her next question. I waved my hand to suggest I'd rather stand.

'We'll need a statement from you, but let's get you sorted out first and we'll be in contact with you, ok?'

With that she stood to one side and I saw the Ambulance crew walk in, who whisked me off to the ambulance. I knew something wasn't right with the jaw, but how severe it was I didn't really know. I laid on the stretcher. I began to feel dizzy and got a sick feeling in the throat. I started to urge. The Paramedic reaches for a cardboard tray for me to spit in to. As I leant over it, I saw blood pouring from my mouth. The reality of the injury and the pain was starting to set in.

I arrived at the hospital at about 10.30pm. It was funny to see the NHS in action meeting with the necessary targets of initial assessments taken place within a set time. Within minutes of being there, I was given the only available cubicle to lay down in. It was the kids' room with some artwork all over the walls of a safari collection of cartoon drawn animals. Typical, I'm not a fan of doctor's surgeries, dentists or hospitals and I got the kid's room. Not bad I thought, getting a cubicle in a few minutes. Laying down in pain and in a lot of discomfort, I was waiting for the initial assessment of injuries. Near on an hour and a half later I got the initial assessment by the duty nurse who gave me a fresh cardboard tray and some fresh tissues. Not so helpful.

Shortly after this I got a visitor. It was my boss from the YMCA. He sat in with me and started chatting. 'Make sure you make a claim for this Neil, it's what our insurance is there for.'

I couldn't really respond too well, but for him a nod was good enough. He sat there for the duration as a welcome support. I felt that I needed to tell him what had happened, but he stopped me.

'No need to tell me now Neil, let's just get you sorted out alright.'

The duty doctor finally turned up at about 12.30am to assess the injuries. The first thing he said was 'There's still a lot of blood here isn't there.' As he started to take a look inside the mouth, I was wincing in pain. 'We're going to need to stop the bleeding, it looks like you have lost a tooth.' He started to make a small roll of padding. Once done he asked 'Can you pop this in your mouth for me to the back right, and bite on it, we need to stop that bleeding.' This hurt loads. I was not liking it, it was the first point that tears began to run, it hurt that much. The doctor then said 'We'll get you in for an x-ray to see if there is any other damage as soon as possible. I'll check these over and come back to you, ok?'

This was shocking. I came in at 10.30pm and at 1.30am, three hours later I got the x-ray. The doctor took about fifteen minutes to check them over and come back to me. 'I have asked a facial specialist to attend and carry out a further assessment and they'll be here shortly.'

At 2.15am the facial specialist arrived after checking the x-rays. 'I have checked the x-rays and it appears Mr Bird, you have a fractured mandible. It will need surgery to fix this. I'll let the duty doctor know and we'll arrange to get you in for admission to get this sorted for you.' I nodded. I was feeling numb at the thought, and exhausted, having fought the pain for a number of hours. The YMCA manager was still with me and was taking all the necessary info in as I continued to feel drowsy. 3.30am and the surgery arrangements at a different hospital were confirmed for admission at 12noon the following day. We left the hospital and prepared for the next day.

Arriving at the hospital where I was to have surgery, they placed me in to a preparation ward for initial assessments and records to be made. As they wheeled me off on the bed to the ward I saw the various ward signs passing my eyes along with the ceiling lights. I saw lights pass then a sign for 'Orthopaedic'. Some lights passed then the next sign 'Urology', more lights and another sign 'Cardiology'. Another set of lights and then another sign, 'Plastic Surgeons Unit'. The trolley bed turned into the ward. At this point I was wondering how bad is it? My stomach started to churn.

After about four days in hospital, I left with two metal plates that were used to fix the jawbone. I had permanent nerve damage due to an impacted tooth, which needed removing. The reason why it had caused so much pain wasn't because I lost a tooth, it was still in there, but it was pushed down into the gum after the daft doctor told me to bite on a bit of pad to try and stop it from bleeding. No wonder it hurt.

"I'VE MADE
A COMPLETE
PIGS EAR
OF THINGS"

'I'VE MADE A COMPLETE PIGS EAR OF THINGS'

11

My first visitors to my house when I returned home from hospital were Alex and Pete, laughing their way into the lounge saying things like 'Where is he then? Man look at the state of you, didn't you punch him back?' and 'Anyone tell you, you look like the elephant man?'

Funny that, this didn't offer me any comfort at all. I'll be honest. I didn't expect any sympathy from these guys. I was sat under a duvet in the recliner armchair with my feet up, I could hardly talk and I dare not laugh as it hurt far too much. I was constantly tired and suffering with pounding headaches. Any movement of the jaw and I could hear this concerning creek. They could see the extent of the injuries and offered their help.

'Give us his name Neil and it'll be sorted,' one of them said.

'He'd have more than a jaw to worry about,' said the other.

I convinced them that I didn't want that to happen, that the Police were involved and he'd have his day in court. But that didn't compute in their heads.

'I don't get it?' said Alex, 'I'd want 'em done over, wouldn't you

Pete?'

Pete knew that it was my say so for the job to go ahead or not.

'Leave it be Alex, Neil if you want us to sort this out, you know you only have to say the word, alright?'

I nodded, but deep down, I didn't want the lad to suffer under the hands of these guys. I'm alive to tell the tale and I knew I'd put myself in the firing line for the knocks when I stood in his way to try and calm him down. If these guys got hold of him, I was worried about what he'd end up getting.

As far as eating was concerned, I wasn't feeling hungry at all to start with. So I ended up getting some fibre nutrient milkshakes to drink. These were ok for a couple of days but I started to feel sick from the large liquid intake and knew I had to start eating soon. I then went on to soft foods for about 6 weeks. You know, there is only so much shepherd's pie a man can enjoy. Mince and mash were most of my meals during this time, oh and yoghurt, something I never really bothered with until then.

My time off work was annoying me somewhat and I seriously wondered about returning to the YMCA. I had to put this down to a one-off event. In the history of the YMCA this was the first major incident in the 15 years I'd known the place. Punches had flown around before between residents, but never caused this kind of damage. There was one incident in the YMCA nationally where a hostel worker died from an unprovoked attack from one of their tenants, which made national news at the time. I came to the conclusion that this shouldn't affect me long term and shouldn't stop me from working there.

The thing that shocked me about this was the lack of support from what was a so-called Christian organisation. In the event of any traumatic experience at work, there was supposed to have been pastoral care provided to help me return to work. I never had any return to work interview or anything because I had started the process for a claim against my employers, who were subsequently instructed not to talk to me about the case. However, this is exactly what was needed. I wanted to understand what had gone wrong and why staff safety was not considered important when bringing in new tenants, as we hadn't been given a full history on his violent nature.

As a legal case this didn't get to Crown Court until April 2005, where Liam was being charged for wounding with intent to cause grievous bodily harm. I was told that the 'intent' charge carried additional weight when sentenced and Liam could face up to 7 years imprisonment. It was during this case that Liam's Police statement was presented to the jury. The Police informed us that, according to his statement, he had drunk three two litre bottles of cider in the space of a couple of hours. He was also a known championship amateur boxer, which would explain the power of the punch. Another argument for the prosecution was that he had a previous conviction for common assault. I have to say the case looked good.

The local newspaper picked up on the Court Case news and plastered this all over the front page of the paper. It read, 'BOXER WENT MAD AT YMCA' in big bold lettering. It was on the A frame boards outside newsagents and everything. This was the main news in our area for a week or so. The first week was announcing the case and the following week was the outcome.

What he got was almost laughable. After two days in court, Liam received 2 years probation and zero fine due to being on benefits. The papers were on the phone to me, begging for a further story, but I didn't give it to them. They wanted to focus on the legal system in our area and the miscarriage of justice. My story wasn't the only one that they could argue. Other local cases were showing the judges up for inconsistencies. At the time of this, I didn't want to get too involved and wanted to keep my head low. What made my story for the papers even stronger, was a local story about a lady trying to stop a robbery in the shop where she worked. She put her hand towards the shop door to go after the lad who had just stolen some stock, the lad slammed the door shut, trapping her hand and breaking it. The lad was put in prison after being charged for the injury to her hand, but for me, to get surgery to my face didn't warrant any imprisonment. The local reporters wanted to highlight this miscarriage of justice and at every opportunity would contact me for comments on a story they were putting together with similar arguments against the Courts.

We often hear the statement 'The law is an ass'. Well being a victim of an assault with evidence as long as your arm, where the lad gets no prison sentence means you can understand why I felt bitter for a time, but knew I had to move on.

I feared for my safety after this time, fearing for repercussions because one of his brothers lived in the same town as me and was regularly seen hanging around outside my home. I don't think the penny ever dropped regarding my identity, but that didn't stop me worrying about it.

My mind was working over time, constantly thinking about what might happen regarding the solicitors dealing with the case for compensation. The Private Investigation work with the potential trouble that can bring and my continued employment with the YMCA. I was doing a lot of thinking.

A few months went by and I spotted the chap who married me to Tina as I was walking through the town centre. I said hello as he walked by. He acknowledged this but then he stopped, taking a good look at me. His name was Rev. Stephen Barks, the Church of England vicar from Wembdon Parish Church.

'Hello, forgive me' he said, 'Remind me'

'Neil... Neil Bird'

'That's it, gotchya!' as he pointed his finger at me.

'Hey how you doing?'

'I'm doing good yeah.' I knew deep down what was going on in my mind, but didn't want to let on too much.

'What is it you do then? What are you up to?' I began to reach for my wallet and pulling out one of my business cards.

'It's not something you would advertise to too many and I doubt you'd ever need my services.'

Looking at the card, his eyes widened with surprise.

'No I don't think I ever would.'

I started to explain the general work, telling him the use of an SLR camera with zoom lenses was all part of the job. Something triggered an idea in his head.

'Are you free next Sunday afternoon? To take some pictures for me? We'd pay you of course.'

'Sure why not, I'd be glad to help out if I can?'

'It's a baptism service and we have a number of our folk being baptised. Could you do us some prints of each person's baptism?'

A week later and I was there with my camera and tripod. I did more than just photos. I had gone away after the event and started on a video presentation. I used the photos with a piece of music in the background, from a Church up north called Abundant Life Church. It was the music they had played on the day. I put a fair bit of time into this and went around to the vicar's house to show him my work. He paid me for the photos and was pleased with them, but the video blew his socks off. Watching it with him almost brought me to tears. The music and images were strong. I started to feel something. I had walked away from my faith as a teenager and become a wreck inside.

He had no clue about any of this. My life as an aggressive chap had finally stopped me in my tracks and I was now finding I was walking around in a daze, with allsorts going on in my head. I lost count of the number of times I would recall the events of the night I took those punches. It wasn't nightmares, but my state of mind was being affected by this daily.

One afternoon at work it got to the point where I was reading the solicitor's paperwork and I sat there and thought, why is this all happening to me? The past couple of years flashed before my eyes. I was divorced from my wife for what appeared to be no real reason at all. I'd got a skin disease that the doctors had no cure for. I was losing my real friends and keeping hold of the friendships that led me towards aggression. But I was finding I was missing the real close friendships I needed at this time. On top of it all, now I was dealing with solicitors, who were assisting me to sue my employers for negligence of health and safety towards their staff, after being attacked and hospitalised. What a crazy couple of years!

I went home at the end of the day and went to my bedroom. I laid on my bed and cried. I cried for near on an hour. I called out to God. 'Why? Why is this all happening?'

It's the naïve question you ask thinking it's everyone else's fault and not yours. After some time I started to realise it was all my doing, I had made some daft decisions in life that had brought me to this desperate point. I had walked away from God as a teenager and I never looked back. I had some basic knowledge of the Bible, which said that Jesus died on the cross for our sins, all that we'd done wrong, and that I could have a personal relationship with him. Thing is, I never truly believed this was possible. For a start he was nowhere to be seen.

At this point I sat up. I took a deep breath, stood up and started to pace around the bedroom.

'Lord, I need you. I can't cope with this anymore?'

I was stood in my bedroom crying and saying sorry repeatedly.

'I've made a complete pigs ear of things... I need your help with this stuff, I can't take it anymore!'

By default I had walked into the devil's path and started to like what I had seen. I prayed aloud.

'If you are there, please clean me Jesus, shield me of these sordid memories and build me back up to the man I'm supposed to be'. I was stood there with my arms up in the air. With all the passion I'd expressed, you would expect lighting bolts or the power in the house to go off or something. Nothing. I brought my arms down and sat back on the bed. I began to pray on every matter of my past that I could. I knew I needed to clear up a lot of stuff and no-one could do this for me, except Jesus. I cried out to God.

'I'm struggling with these feelings inside'

For those of you reading this from a non-Christian viewpoint, don't get freaked out. If you have never prayed in your life before, don't panic. If you have found yourself praying but feel you get no answer, same here, because for me, it didn't happen over night. It's like taking your car for the MOT but not giving them your car to even look at. If you don't give the garage the car to look at, how can you expect to receive the MOT certificate? If you don't give Jesus your heart and your all, how can you expect Him to repair you? To answer the cry of your heart or to grant you the relationship with Him that you ask for?

For God to change me and work in my life, it meant being open to Him. I couldn't do it half-hearted. I had to give him my all. However, to do this had a high level of vulnerability, exposing the parts of me not even those closest to me knew. I had to hand everything over that I didn't want any longer and that was doing me no good.

I didn't get a lightening bolt experience. You ask any Christian and not many do. However, within a short space of time, there was a load of jargon that I was beginning to understand. The first was the word 'faith', which I learned was about a belief in the seemingly invisible. I had to change the way I thought about my belief in Jesus. I had to understand that it took faith to truly believe in the supernatural. Another word I had to learn the true meaning of was 'grace'. I never truly knew what this meant. Up until now it was religious mumbo-jumbo that I never really had an understanding of. Without searching for the answer from the Bible or a dictionary, in my head was the answer. Something I never knew before was now answered in my head? Grace was what Jesus had over my life, an acceptance of me no matter what my past looked like. My life needed a rewind and erase button, this is what His grace did. When I sought forgiveness of my messed up life, there appeared His grace. A grace that saved me, accepted me as I was and cleaned me up, regardless of the stench of my past. Wow, I never got that lightening bolt but what I got was a slow understanding of the things He was doing in my life. There wasn't an instant reaction, but there was a transformation happening.

Throughout my life I had moved home around eleven or twelve times and one thing had managed to follow me around, without getting lost. It was my King James Version of the Bible, a small pocket version. I had lost the majority of my belongings from the last move because I didn't consider them important to me and left them all behind for Tina to clear out. But the Bible, since I was 8 years old, I still had? I started to read the Gospels in search of the meaning of the cross. In John chapter 10 verse 10 the Message Bible reads, 'A thief is only there to steal and kill and destroy. I came so they can have real and eternal life, more and better life than they ever dreamed of.'

I was starting to understand that a spiritual battle for my soul, the core of who I am, was going on. On a day-to-day basis I was having battles over decisions and actions. It wasn't an overnight transformation, it was the start of a journey that meant me making decisions each day to live the life God wanted for me. Although the battles were tough, I knew that ultimately God had won the war and I was now seeking a better path for my life.

A few weeks went by and I had now been attending regularly at the Church that Stephen was the vicar of. This was now the building of my new life. I had made the re-commitment from my teenage years to come back to Jesus and put Him first, but this time I knew it felt different. This was a real commitment for something different. I started to make new friends who were a true encouragement to me.

After a sermon one Sunday, I remember Stephen preaching on the friends in our world outside Church, who may not be helping in our relationship with Jesus and living the kind of life we should. This hit me full on. I was still connected with my buddies who I knew had a different way of life to me and was pulling me down their path. It wasn't that I started to dislike them, I just knew I had to distance myself from them and focus on building my relationship with Jesus, which I couldn't do with these guys so closely around. I built up the courage to tell them that I was going to Church and my focus on life had to change from the old ways. They laughed it off at first but started to realise what this meant and that I was serious. 'You mean, you're ditching us for some poncey Church folk' said Alex with a slight aggression in his voice.

'I have to, I can't be around here anymore.'

It was painful to do, and not easy at all. With these kind of guys you build up a trust level and a respect level that in their world is difficult to break. I was now walking away from this. Even though I knew it was for the best, they couldn't see it, and assumed I was joining some kind of cult or something. Not a nice thing to do, but something that needed to happen. Hopefully one day I would be able to have them in my world again, even if not so close. Since this day, I started to visit other Christian homes and enjoy a different kind of cup of coffee, a time that may have included prayer and support, with people who wanted the best for me.

I found that there were some other things holding me back from moving forward. I understood what I thought was necessary to have a full on relationship with Jesus, but there was a stumbling block. It was another word that for some is just Churchy jargon. Forgiveness. This was what I thought Jesus did for me, through His grace. I didn't realise that I had to forgive others too. It was another sermon message about the forgiveness of others that struck a chord with me. I had my relation's killer and my attacker to think about here. Ok, I could understand what I needed to do it wasn't rocket science I thought. I decided I would pray for forgiveness of their actions and actively work out this problem. I'd never really prayed much before and so unsure of how to really do it or what I was meant to say I prayed.

'Lord, help me to forgive these two lads, I don't know how I can, but I know you can help me understand how to?'

It's weird how when you ask for something like true forgiveness, God answers your prayers. It wasn't bolts of lightening or deep voices from the skies above. On this occasion for me it was the change in feelings towards the lads. The bitterness left me and I began to get a different understanding on things. As for my attacker, he didn't know me or attack me because of anything personal. It could have just as easily been Jeanette who took the blows to the head. I now began to think that my build, size and ability to restrain him afterwards, was God putting me in that situation to take the blows. A more fragile person may have received the blows and it could have been fatal. At least I was alive to tell the tale.

Something else was there, but it was deeper to search for. I needed to forgive my ex-wife, Tina, who wanted to break up the marriage. Being a private investigator, I had been searching stuff out and asking people for info, searching online for any news and looking for anything that would confirm my fears that she had another bloke. Within a year I had found out what I needed to know, she was in a relationship with a guy who had filled my shoes. Yet I was still struggling, I would avoid being in the same room as the opposite sex on my own, because I wasn't ready to move on. I had come to a point where I needed closure and the only real way to get this was by forgiving her for her actions. Behind closed doors I would shed a tear, but knew I had to now let go of this in order for God to take me to the next phase in my journey with Him and to move on to the new things he had in store for me.

When you discover the meaning of the Bible and it's purpose as a communication tool from God to you, you begin to have a thirst to get stuck in and read more. If you're a person who doesn't read much, you'll dip in and out reading a verse or two at a time. This was me I was never a big reader.

It was August 2005 and I heard Stephen mention a verse during one of his sermons. This same verse was one I had read earlier that week and it came from Revelation chapter 3 verse 20. In the verse Jesus said, 'Look at me. I stand at the door. I knock. If you hear me call and open the door, I'll come right in and sit down to supper with you'.

I have never read a book from cover to cover in my life and the Bible certainly didn't have the necessary appeal to start. It was far too complicated for me to take on as a first book. When God wants to communicate something to you, He'll make sure you get the message even if you don't read much.

In November, a few of the men from the Church were off to a men's conference at the Abundant Life Church in Bradford. I'm going to keep this short because I don't remember much of it. All I remember is coming back thinking, 'well that was nice'. In reality it was two and a half days of sitting down listening to preachers. Some of it was good, but the majority of it was motivational thinking about taking a stand in Church, being real men, standing up and being noticed in the Church. They meant well, but they'd never met the controlling women we had in our Church back home. Us lot walking in to our Church and throwing our weight around was never going to go down well and as you'd expect, when we went back with a fizz, it soon fizzled out and we were back to square one.

My faith and belief didn't take a knock, but these conferences never really floated my boat at all. In my late teens I often went to conferences working behind the scenes and would often meet the guest speakers. The only ones I had met appeared to have split personalities when on and off the stage. I had a sceptical view on conferences and hid my feelings on the matter when I returned home, but I remember thinking, this is exactly what I had expected. Zero impact. This was the missed opportunity to get something that God had longed for in my life. The message of being a lion for Jesus in our hometowns was about being strong men of God and strong leaders. I had completely missed the point.

Another hurdle in my life that I had to jump over was the investigation business. I had to let it go. It had been going about twenty months and it was now time to come to a close. The other two guys had been in employment for a while now and in effect I had become a sole trader, with them no longer having an interest in the business. What appeared to be a great business developing in Bridgwater was not the best occupation to be in. I had come to the conclusion that I no longer wanted to earn my living assisting solicitors in cases that supported divorce. To gain evidence on cheating husbands was slapping me in the face that none of this was God's will for me, nor the people I was investigating. The majority of investigation cases were matrimonial and the irretrievable breakdown of marriages was becoming an epidemic. The UK, at the time, had one of the highest divorce rates in Europe. I ceased the business in February 2006 and began a media business that used photography as a main source of income. Weddings were to be the main focus for good income and the jobs started to come in. I changed my business address and set up a photography studio for family portraits.

There's a known saying that the greatest trick the devil ever pulled was convincing the world Jesus never existed. I knew God had radically changed my life. I would have been six foot under if I'd followed the devil's plan for my life. I had been falling into a violent world where nothing scared me or I'd react without thinking first. It was a path that would have led to getting caught by the police, injured, or even worse killed, heading towards hell without 'passing go or collecting £200'.

God had helped me clean up my life, my relationships and my work. My Church life moved along slowly and I began to get myself more involved with the life of the Church. But the next season was approaching fast and it was something I wasn't at all expecting. It was something I was trying to avoid, but when God wants you to do something, He has a way of letting you know... repeatedly.

'IT DOESN'T MEAN BECOMING A WUSS'

'IT DOESN'T MEAN BECOMING A WUSS'

12

As we headed towards Christmas I got a job that stretched my media skills. This was with the youth of the Church, filming a modern day nativity. The filming and editing went well and we were ready for the nativity service one December evening. The service had the younger kids doing the usual traditional style, teacloth on the head, nativity scenes, but in between each part the congregation watched a film clip of the same scene but in a modern style from the youth group.

Half the congregation laughed out loud when they saw sketches from the famous British comedy, Little Britain influencing the youth's version of the nativity story. No room at the inn, turned into Margaret's shop, the Scottish hotel owner and 'The computer says no' sketches. The other half who had never seen the TV comedy still found it somewhat amusing and thought we had worked on an amazing script. It was a great piece of work and fun to do. I had been at the Church for six months and I was enjoying using my media skills to help them.

I went through the next six months quite happy with the

Church family and getting myself involved in all things 'churchy'. This included quiz nights, Sunday lunches and special occasion evenings. My media influence was changing the way people did Church.

It was about this time that one of the oldies spoke to me quietly after a Sunday service. 'We have a vacancy on the PCC, the Church management committee, and you'd be an asset on the committee. What do you think?'

I didn't even stop to think. 'Nope, not for me, thanks for asking but I don't do committees, think they're a waste of time.' In my head I thought 'like I'd be part of any change in this place.' The ones who sat on the committee were a stubborn minded lot and I thought I'd be wasting my time trying. It would have been like talking to a brick wall. I put a stop to his ideas of me joining them.

Why is it that people always like the feeling of power or control on things? The only thing I wanted to be a part of was change, because to be static for me meant to be boring. You always have to keep moving with stuff. The sound guy would often get told to turn down the sound levels in Church because it was too loud. When the complainers backs were turned, I'd lean over and try and creep the faders up again. I wanted a powerful impact at Church and if people had hearing aids that were causing trouble because it was too loud, I thought they should turn themselves down or take them off!

I turned up to Church and took the laptop to plug into the projector, for some video work one Sunday. I'd forgotten the DVD disc, which I'd left in the car. So I headed out to the car park. The sound guy, Paul, and his wife pulled up and I saw 'the fish' logo newly stuck to the back of their car. I had an understanding, whether right or wrong about these things, which was that the fish needed to point to the left. If the head pointed to the right is suggested it was going with the flow of the others, but pointing to the left suggested going against the flow and in a biblical sense taking the narrow road instead of the broad road. I told them this but then expressed my views on it.

'I don't get why you want to put one of them on your motor anyway?'

'We like it, don't you?'

'No, you wouldn't catch me putting one of them on my motor!'

'Probably not, because you don't want people to know you're a Christian when you cut them up or slam on your horn because they did the same to you' Paul replied with a mild chuckle.

'I don't know what you mean' I said with a smirk. 'But you're right.'

His wife chipped in and said with a smile 'I'm going to get you one and we'll put it on your car without you knowing.'

'Don't even think about it, if I spot it on my motor, I'll be taking it off straight away and slinging it.'

'Even if I bought it for you?' she said

'Without hesitation, don't even think about it, I'm not having that tat on my motor.'

They were laughing walking into Church that day. I was thinking to myself, I hope they don't even try.

A week or so went by and I was in Church again, and a friendly face called Mary handed me an envelope with a smile. 'Thought this may be of interest to you?' she said.

I acknowledge this with a 'Thanks' and continued to set up the techie stuff at the back of the Church. Once done, I opened the envelope. It was a brochure for the next conference at that Abundant Life Church, called 'Stronger 2006'. I didn't know why she had passed it to me. My understanding was that this was a conference for leaders of the Church.

'Mary, this is for leaders in the Church, and I'm not one.'

'Thought you may be interested and you're part of the team here.'

'No, it's not for me, do you want this back?' as I popped the brochure back into the envelope.

'Take it home and have a read of it, if you're not interested pop it in the bin,' walking away talking to someone else.

As I turned around, I thought 'I'll find a bin now then.' I wasn't going, it was for leaders of the Church and I wasn't one nor did I intend to be one.

The following Sunday, Stephen's wife Rosemary walked up to me with a beaming smile. 'I hear you're coming with us.'

'Where's that then?' I replied

'To Stronger' she smiled.

'No, Mary asked me last week, but I said no, it wasn't for me, it's for the leaders in the Church'

'Oh' the smile dropped into a confused look.

'I may have got it wrong or misheard something. I thought you were coming?'

'No not me' I said and she walked away to catch up with someone else.

During the week I got a phone call, this time from Stephen.

'Hiya, a little birdie tells me you're joining us at Stronger'.

Here we go again, I thought, what is this? 'No, who is this little birdie, because whoever talks to me I keep saying no, I have never said yes, Stronger in my understanding is for leaders and I have no thoughts of being one in the Church especially this one.'

'Well it's not for leaders as such, it's for those who play a valued part in the Church and you are one of them.'

I declined one more time and said 'I'll come along to the Xcel Men's Conference in November instead.'

On Stephen's return from Stronger, he attended a PCC meeting and the long and the short of it, was he walked out of the meeting throwing in the towel and beginning to prepare his exit from his position in the Church of England. He'd had enough with the whole thing, every change he wanted to bring in was being brick walled. The full story is Stephen's to share. I'll just say that this didn't stop a core group of four men supporting him and attending the upcoming men's conference.

November arrived and I wasn't sure I could afford to go. My finances were rock bottom and a job owing a few hundred quid hadn't paid up. I told Paul, that the cost was a deciding factor for me as to whether I could go or not. He agreed saying 'If you don't go, I may not go either'. Days before the conference it was still an unknown. I said to him, 'If God wants us there, He'll get us there aye?'

The day before I had a cheque clear in the bank and we could go. I phoned Paul. 'Hey Paul, you still up for going? I have the cash now and can do it?'

'Yeah can do', he said.

So we arranged the necessary plans and we went to the conference.

Paul wasn't your typical Christian. Don't be fooled by the fact that he stuck a fish on his car. He had a past, like all of us and wasn't your stereotypical Church-goer. Like me, he was a bloke's bloke and we both got on well, learning as we went along.

This was the conference that rocked my world. God got me there because he wanted to tell me something. Remember I said that if God wants you to know something it often comes in repetition, well this was blatantly obvious.

I walked into the resources shop, turned to Paul and said 'I'm gonna get myself a new Bible. I feel the need to get one that's easier to read.'

'Ok, I'll go and grab a coffee and find a table and see you in a mo.'

I was stood in the resources shop for a good five to ten minutes looking at the various versions. One stood out. It was a leather bound Bible, and when I flicked through the pages it had supporting notes referring to characters in the Bible. It also had a nice page layout, which appealed to me. I had no idea how much it was and the cover was plain black. I took it up to the counter and the staff member said, 'There's a box to go with this one, hang on, it's under here somewhere'. They ducked behind the counter popped the Bible into the box and placed it into a carrier bag.

'That's £39.99.'

How much? Rattled in my head.

'Sure that's fine,' passing her the magic plastic card from my wallet. I reluctantly thought it would be a good investment. I also didn't want the embarrassment of walking away from the till saying I couldn't afford it.

I walked into the café area and found Paul. I sat with him, opened up the box and pulled out the Bible. He was on the phone to his wife, telling her we had got there safely. I opened up the first couple of pages and saw something that made me close it abruptly and shove it back into the bag.

'I don't believe it!'

'What's that?' Paul questioned. I explained the repetition thing to him that when God is trying to tell you something it keeps coming up. He agreed that he knew this happened. I then opened the bag and pulled out the Bible again to reveal the box saying 'Maxwell's Leadership Bible'. I was getting a clear message from Him. I had bought a Bible and didn't even look at what I had bought until after I had paid for it.

Paul laughed and said, 'Think He's trying to tell you something.'

I was puzzled during the day as to what I was supposed to do with this insight. Later that day the guest speaker Paul De Yong spoke about taking on the challenges that face us. I was sat in the auditorium puzzled, I was feeling a bit odd, and started to look around the building from where I was sat. I could see the café area, which had a glazed balcony and I had a picture in my head, of me cleaning it. I turned back and looked at the carpet in front of me. What was that? I turned back to look at the glass and saw me stood there leaning over and cleaning the glass, looking at me and waving at me. What did this mean? I had no clue. Firstly what was the meaning of cleaning and why here? In my old life, I'd have laughed at what had just happened saying I'd drunk too much or was hallucinating. I just knew this was God.

That evening I saw a member of the conference staff that I recognised. I told them that I bought a new Bible and they offered to take it and try to get a staff discount for me. They took the box but not the Bible, as I wanted to use it over the course of the conference. The following day, the staff member handed me back the box, but there was some stuff in it 'What've you put inside?'

'Oh nothing much' they said.   'Just a few things I thought might be of interest'.

As I opened the box, I looked up at them and said, 'You're just having a laugh aren't you?'

They looked over to me and said, 'What's that?'

I had opened the box and the first thing I saw in there was a brochure for the Church's Bible school, titled The Abundant Life Leadership Academy. They looked at what I had shown them.

'You bet,' they said and walked away leaving me a bit bewildered.

This person was currently doing the course at the Church and this was their subtle way of recommending it to me. I was getting multiple messages from all angles. Leadership messages in July, August, September and now November. I had got the point, but had no clue why or what for?

It wasn't until I drove home with Paul that I began to realise what God was calling me to do. I was listening to a teaching CD I had bought at the conference by the Abundant Life Church Pastor, Paul Scanlon who was talking about relevant Churches vs. relic, traditional religious types which are on offer to many. He spoke about the Churches of today needing to be relevant for the people of today or they'll end up as relics and museums for tourists to visit. This shouted volumes to me. I knew Stephen had a passion for a relevant Church with a new focus to reach out into the community. Two sayings came to me and I'm not sure where from. When I arrived back in Bridgwater after a long journey home, I dropped Paul off and drove straight to Stephen's home. I knocked on his door hoping he had arrived back home. He opened the door and I said 'I'm not sure where it says it in the Bible but I have two verses going over and over in my head.'

'Go on.'

'Old men dream dreams and young men shall see visions, I have seen things this weekend that I need to tell you about. The other one is this, write the vision down and he that reads it will run with it, I have no idea where they come from, I'm sure you can tell me'.

Without hesitation he replied, 'The first one is from Acts chapter 2 verse 17 and the other one is from one of the prophets in the Old Testament, Habakkuk somewhere?' He cracked a tear in the eye as I did the same. This seemed like a moment in time that was about to change our future relationship. He took a step back, gestured a welcome arm 'Come on in, I think we need to have a natter don't we?'

From that day, things changed and we birthed, with the new appointed leader Richard Brummitt, what is now known as Alive Christian Ministries. The next book to be written will tell you more about Alive, the history of how it got started and the hurdles we had to jump in order to grow as a Church. We felt it was the time for something different in the south west of England. We had Stephen's dream for a 21st century Church, but as a team under new leadership we were now about to make this a reality. Alive needed to be a Church that had a heart for people especially those not already effectively reached in our local area. This was what the leadership signs had been pointing me towards. Who would have guessed it, God wanted to use someone like me with my background to help to lead a Church!

So, why this book? Why did I want to tell people the story of this huge transformation in my life?

Many people are trapped in a lifestyle of violence. Mindless violence has claimed the lives of many doormen. Being stabbed or shot is always a living fear in the back of any doorman's mind.

Sadly this is more and more common for many men in this world. A world of violence is difficult to get out of unhurt. Either you end up in prison, battered beyond recognition or more tragically lying in a pool of your own blood… dead.

You can't trust anyone, not even your so-called mates. You have to constantly watch your own back, always worrying about repercussions. You don't want anyone knowing where you live because you fear that violence will be brought to the house affecting those you live with. You live in fear, that's why many take the 'hit first' mentality.

I'm making a step to reach these guys and anyone who reads the book to say, there is a fire exit. It's lit up and Jesus is waiting by the door for you.

Whenever we go somewhere new, we all get to know the fire procedures of the building for health and safety reasons. We all know the direction and escape routes, but you have these have-a-go heroes trying to put the inferno out single-handed. You can't put satan out with a bit of water, he's ablaze and gonna be burning for some time. There's nothing you or anyone else can do to tame him, his rage is getting worse. His purpose is to steal, destroy and kill anything good in your life. Get out while you can, get out of the old destructive life and into a new life, Jesus is waiting for you. Hmmm…. Went off on one there. Nice analogy though.

The statistics from the Institute of Alcohol Studies regarding alcohol related violence shows a definite link with the binge drinking culture we are currently in. Southampton, where I worked on the doors, is situated in one the highest counties listed for drink related violent offences.

I'd like to think of myself as living proof that Jesus is alive and is still changing lives today. His grace is sufficient, His forgiveness breathed life in me again. I'd always believed there was a God and that Jesus died for my sins, but for me, like the child in me, I had to make mistakes to learn everything that Jesus did for me, was true. Who hasn't learnt from their mistakes? Some would argue it's the best way of learning, because you get a true feeling of His grace, forgiveness, faith, love and His spirit.

I want to share the message that we live in a violent world but you don't have to be a part of that violence, by speaking to groups, prisons or Churches. I want you to learn from my mistakes so you don't have to go down the same road. I want to use this book as a foot in the door in situations where I can challenge men to think differently about their lives. I want to help people escape the world of violence.

You have picked this book up for a reason, so as the reader I'm speaking to you too. If you don't know that Jesus has a better way for your life then read on and discover what He has done and can continue to do for you.

Jesus died for all our sins and He is ready to give anyone who comes to Him, a fresh start, a clean slate and a better future. Don't worry, that doesn't mean becoming a wuss or the typical Christian guy portrayed on the TV. He wants you to come to Him as you, warts and all, pardon the expression.

For me, Jesus has brought me to a place of peace, calmness and stability. The fear of repercussions has left me. The fear of people has changed into a compassion for those in need.

People are the reason I'm here. This book and the chance to share my story, is an opportunity to go back into situations where I will meet violent aggressive men. I am now using my story to bring hope to those who need a change of direction. From a path of darkness to a path filled with light, a path of hope, faith and life.

In Matthew chapter 28 verse 19, the great commission tells us to 'make disciples of all the nations, baptising them in the name of the Father, Son and Holy Spirit'. In the Message version of the Bible it reads, 'Jesus, undeterred, went right ahead and gave his charge: God authorized and commanded me to commission you. Go out and train everyone you meet, far and near, in this way of life, marking them by baptism in the threefold name; Father, Son, and Holy Spirit. Then instruct them in the practice of all I have commanded you. I'll be with you as you do this, day after day after day, right up to the end of the age'.

Reaching those 'far and near', we need to think about reaching the people in our world. This includes, the abused, the vulnerable, the needy and the violent too. God loves them and wants us, as Christians, to reach out to help them. So, if you're a Christian I hope this book has opened your eyes to the people you are reaching out to and including in your world. You may never know what amazing things are locked up inside the people you pass by each day.

If you're someone who's not thought about God before and you're breathing, then it's not too late to think about a different life. Don't let pride get in the way of you taking steps towards making a change.

What God has got planned next for my life, who knows? If He can take me on a journey from working in a world of violence, being divorced and attacked to healing my life and playing my part in leading a Church, then there is nothing that is impossible to Him. What I do know is that I am loving every minute of it.

"AND FINALLY..."

'BEFORE WE DRAW THE RAFFLE IT'S TIME TO CUT THE CAKE'

My Dad would call this phrase out anywhere to draw attention, so it seems fitting to bring it up here for the quick thank you speech.

Firstly, thank you to my parents, **Colin Bird** & **Eve Puddy**. I have had a great life and your support continues to be a huge encouragement. I know the future is brighter and at some point, when it is possible, I will return all the favours and loans over the many years of getting me to where I am today. But for now, it's ONE BIG THANK YOU to you both.

I'd like to thank the lads in the photo for Chapter 3, **Mark, Luis, Peter, Magnus, Rob** & **Karl**. Many more were taken at the time and are shown regularly as part of the Never Been Punched Presentation. I'd also like to thank **Toks**, for the photo for Chapter 6.

Thank you to the two writers who were an inspiration to me. **Allie Outram** & **George McMullen**. Thank you for your encouragement and direction during the early stages.

Thank you to **the lads in the Caffé Nero**, Taunton, who constantly kept me going on caffeine whilst writing the book, which seemed to speed up, as the stronger coffee kicked in. Hope you've reserved my regular seat for the writing of book two.

Thanks also go to two blokes, **Arthur White** & **Matt Stockdale** for taking time to read the review copy of the book before getting the book published. Your support in helping a first time author is very much appreciated. I pray our relationship continues to open doors for each of our ministries.

A very special thank you goes to **Joanne Wardman**, my fiancé. As I wrote this book, we were going out together and now we're engaged. Probably by the time some of you get to read this we'll be married. Joe (yes spelt with an 'e') has been a huge help in getting this book in the readable condition it is today. I also need to let the reader know that some of the images used in this book and the ones in the Never Been Punched Presentation were taken by Joe.

Thank you for your patience and kindness in the last few months and helping me finish off this book. I love you so much and I can't wait to spend a happy 'God Filled' life together.

And finally one apology. It was an unintentional oversight that I neglected to mention my brother, **Jason Bird**, in the book. If I don't mention him I'm liable to never get my holiday apartment in Malta ever again. So, hey Jas' thanks for being the Big Bro, man you're the best. You're the only one, which also means I have nothing to compare you to, but hey, I got you in the book, now you owe me a pint. See you soon.

'CHEERS GUYS!'